The [No-Nonsense Guide to]

WORLD POVERTY

'Publishers have created lists of short books that discuss the questions that your average [electoral] candidate will only ever touch if armed with a slogan and a soundbite. Together [such books] hint at a resurgence of the grand educational tradition... Closest to the hot headline issues are *The No-Nonsense Guides*. These target those topics that a large army of voters care about, but that politicos evade. Arguments, figures and documents combine to prove that good journalism is far too important to be left to (most) journalists.'

Boyd Tonkin,
The Independent,
London

To the memory of Winin Pereira, dear friend and teacher, in homage and affection.

About the author
Jeremy Seabrook has written more than 30 books, including *Freedom Unfinished, Children of Other Worlds, Love in a Different Climate* and *Colonies of the Heart*. He has been a teacher, social worker and lecturer, and has written plays for theater, TV and radio. He has contributed to many journals and newspapers, including the **New Internationalist**, Third World Network, *New Statesman* and *The Ecologist*, and at present writes for *The Statesman* in Kolkata (Calcutta).

Acknowledgements
All the people in the poor places of the world from whom I have learned so much about injustice but also hope in the world.

Other titles in the series
The No-Nonsense Guide to Animal Rights
The No-Nonsense Guide to Climate Change
The No-Nonsense Guide to Conflict and Peace
The No-Nonsense Guide to Fair Trade
The No-Nonsense Guide to Globalization
The No-Nonsense Guide to Global Health
The No-Nonsense Guide to Human Rights
The No-Nonsense Guide to International Development
The No-Nonsense Guide to Islam
The No-Nonsense Guide to Science
The No-Nonsense Guide to Sexual Diversity
The No-Nonsense Guide to Tourism
The No-Nonsense Guide to World History

About the New Internationalist
The **New Internationalist** is an independent not-for-profit publishing co-operative. Our mission is to report on issues of global justice. We publish informative current affairs and popular reference titles, complemented by world food, photography and gift books as well as calendars, diaries, maps and posters – all with a global justice world view.

If you like this *No-Nonsense Guide* you'll also love the **New Internationalist** magazine. Each month it takes a different subject such as *Trade Justice, Nuclear Power* or *Iraq*, exploring and explaining the issues in a concise way; the magazine is full of photos, charts and graphs as well as music, film and book reviews, country profiles, interviews and news.

To find out more about the **New Internationalist**, visit our website at
www.newint.org

The **NO-NONSENSE GUIDE** to
WORLD POVERTY

Jeremy Seabrook

The No-Nonsense Guide to World Poverty
Published in the UK by
New Internationalist™ Publications Ltd
Oxford OX4 1BW, UK
www.newint.org
New Internationalist is a registered trade mark.

First published 2003; second edition 2007.

Cover image: Chris Stowers/Panos Pictures

Series editor: Troth Wells
Design by New Internationalist Publications Ltd.

 Printed on recycled paper by TJ International Ltd, Padstow, Cornwall, UK
who hold environmental accreditation ISO 14001.

British Library Cataloguing-in-Publication Data.
A catalogue record for this book is available from the British Library.

Library of Congress Cataloguing-in-Publication Data.
A catalogue for this book is available from the Library of Congress.

ISBN: 978-1-904456-66-7

The strength of the *No-Nonsense* series is that it lives up to its name. The authors, not specialists but educated observers, seek to simplify vast, complicated problems and broaden the scope of people who want to read between the headlines of the morning paper. The issues described in each book often overlap, stimulating readers to connect rising temperatures, US workers' concerns about immigration, the instability of the stock market, the overhaul of the US military and the coffee we drink.

The *Guides* are no-frills introductions to expanding dialogues in international politics. But these small yet mighty volumes prove that a basic grasp of current events helps empower us to mobilize as citizens of the world and consumers against the status quo.

Michelle Chen
War Resisters League
www.warresisters.org

CONTENTS

Introduction

THE FIRST TIME I went to India I visited an industrial slum in Mumbai (Bombay). Here I met workers in companies that were subcontracted to transnational corporations. It was a great shock, not because this was some strange and outlandish experience, but because it recalled to me the conditions in which my family had lived and worked, throughout the 19th and early 20th century, in an industrial town in the English Midlands.

It was a shock of recognition. My visits to Mumbai and later to many other cities in the South – Jakarta, Dhaka, São Paulo – were not to foreign places. It was like going home. Another climate, a different people, a separate culture; these were nothing compared to the sameness of poverty. Poor people are always poor in the same way.

In Dhaka, Bangladesh, seeing young girls of 12 and 13 cutting the loose threads on finished garments reminded me of my mother and her sisters. At the same age they had begun knot-tying in shoe factories, sitting beneath the benches, their nimble fingers proving so useful in tying the ends of threads so that they would not fray. The scenes of factory life were like a trip though time to the demolished sites of manufacture in the West, now re-established elsewhere – making the same basic necessities which were the staple occupation of the great majority of towns and cities of Britain in the generations after the Industrial Revolution. Even the stories of survival were familiar to me from those told by older members of my family: waiting for the day's wages in order to go and buy food for the evening meal; sifting through the waste at the end of market day to find a few specked oranges and mildewed tomatoes from which to salvage some nutrition; standing in line at the baker's shop in the early morning to take the pick of stale bread and pastries; living in fear of the moneylender and the pawnbroker; leaving the house by night to avoid paying rent to the landlord; arbitrary employers who thought nothing of swearing at, even beating, young women workers who made mistakes at their work; being dismissed for trying to organize; bewilderment and insecurity in the presence of officials; children scavenging for old bottles, rags and rabbit skins to make a few coins out of waste.

The echoes of life between North and South have even deeper resonances. Further back in history the enclosures of the commons and the degradation of rural life evicted people in Britain from agriculture and sent them to seek shelter in the manufacturing towns. The pressure on small and subsistence farmers in the South today is identical; the sorrowful departures from the home-place on migrations to towns and cities in search of a livelihood which the landscapes of home can no longer supply – how globalization has expanded these journeys of hope, away from agriculture and self-reliance towards the grudging shelters of the expanding cities of the South.

Poverty, resistance, the ingenuity of survivors, the self-sacrifice of women, the unending search for a better life – these things are not new in the world. With urbanization and 'modernization' people meet new forms of poverty – the drug-dealer and the gun, addictions and violence, in the *favela* and the *barrio* as well as the public-housing schemes of North America and Europe. These give a new urgency to the search for a common, global solidarity between poor people in their search, not for riches but for security and sufficiency. These simple aims have everywhere been smothered by the economic imperative of constant growth and the compulsion of 'more', rather than what constitutes enough for daily needs.

Jeremy Seabrook
London

1 The invisible poor

A vanishing trick has been performed in the rich world. This makes poor people harder to see in the rest of the world as well – where the very modesty of their demands drowns out their voices.

'The poverty of our century is unlike that of any other. It is not, as poverty was before, the result of natural scarcity, but of a set of priorities imposed upon the rest of the world by the rich. Consequently, the modern poor are not pitied... but written off as trash.'
John Berger, cultural critic

IN THE RICH world the poor have become invisible. The spaces they occupy remain uncolonized by the rich. Poor people have only walk-on parts in the great drama of progress narrated by the selective imagery of global communications conglomerates. Poor people make an appearance in international news programs mainly as scarecrows or as a stimulus to charity.

The US and Europe have performed a vanishing trick on their own poor. They are now contained in statistics until they erupt in spectacular crimes, riots, racial disturbances, police raids on the houses of drug dealers, football hooligans. They are not part of mainstream society, which is prosperous, busy and buoyant.

The Western poor are the dead souls of democracy: non-participants, dropped out and disappeared, unregistered, slipped off electoral rolls and official lists; fly-by-nights, the transients who leave no trace; the rejected elderly, old people sitting behind closed curtains in the high-summer days, falling asleep over afternoon TV, while a bird twitters in its cage.

Dead souls are the outcasts of the market, the discounted who don't count, consoled by the lottery ticket and the disoccupational therapy of the book of puzzles, reading cartoons in the tabloids on the formica top of the café table. Dead souls are hustlers and survivors, economic shadows in the shadow economy, the discouraged and despairing who have fallen through the bottom line of accounting systems; servicers of obscure desires, dancers in attendance on the illicit needs aroused by a culture of wanting, the providers of underage sex, snuff movies, the dealers in substances that alter minds already changed too often.

The nowhere addresses of rejected seekers of asylum are on the inner ring-roads of German cities, the exurban slums of Paris and Marseilles, the periphery of Turin and Milan, Victorian properties in North London; where plastic buckets catch water from leaky roofs, the smell of unwashed shirts and sweaty feet, rags stuffed into warped windowpanes to keep out the drafts, low-watt bulbs shimmering on lumpy piss-flowered mattresses, the mushroom of breath in gassy bathrooms; the refuges of the lost, the missing in inaction.

Of the 100,000 teenage runaways in Britain each year, more than a quarter have run away at least three times; 18,000 are turned out by their parents. Adults, too, walk out on relationships, a scribbled note on the table saying they can't stand it any longer; 50 per cent of deserting fathers lose contact with their children within two years.

Joanne and Kath

In their mid-thirties, they met sleeping rough in the Victoria area of London. Now they share a hostel room. On the concourse of the mainline station, they drink cider (5-per-cent proof, $3 a bottle), discussing what made Kath put her fist through a window last night. 'You only got a fucking scratch.' 'I'd rather hurt myself than hurt you.' Both wear denim, Joanne from Devon, Kath from South London. 'She's my partner,' says Kath, proud of a word that seems to give substance to their relationship. 'We take life a day at a time.' Kath hasn't seen her family since her mother died, Joanne doesn't know where her sisters are. 'I heard my Mum was in New Cross. I went there, but nobody had heard of her.' ■

The invisible poor

There is a thriving market in identities, transformed appearances, forged papers, fake birth certificates, false marriages and the assumption of the persona of the dead: businesses devoted to the adult truancies of citizenship. People become someone else to run up debt, go on a stolen credit-card spree, leaving the discarded purse and empty wallet in the waste-bin.

Those who have fallen through safety-nets and have sustained psychological injuries, emotional derangement, the homeless on the waste ground with their cylinders of beer and faces illuminated by smoky fires burning plastic and wood under the railway bridges; spirit worn away by drugs, the intentless loiterers in the dark.

Young men and women in cracked plastic coats, smelly dogs on a chain begging outside a civic center; street vendors of fake Nina Ricci, Gucci and Rolex, set out on a piece of Astroturf which they bundle up like a conjurer when the police appear; young black boys, devotees of the cargo cults of shopping malls, distant descendants of slaves enslaved now to multinational logos, which also enslave young women working in the lightless suburbs of Asian cities; the sellers of contraband Marlboros, the spotty complexion of Eastern European malnourishment. The tranquilized whose eyes speak of passions doused by chemicals; distraught women who thrust leaflets published in Lebanon, Ohio, announcing that Satan Rules the World, the old woman in a dressing gown who no longer knows where she lives; people chased out of their mind by the reason of an irrational world.

There are whole zones of dead souls, the charity-clad on windy housing estates, grass trampled by half-wild dogs and snot-nosed children, broken saplings, baby-buggies and plastic bags, high-rise, low-esteem people standing in line for handouts, or the benefit of the doubts of wealth.

Gus

'I spent seven years on the streets after prison. I done my first robbery at 17. With Frankie Fraser, we done a jeweler's in Bond Street. I was the driver. Goods worth £25,000 ($40,000). I got £200 ($320). I was with the Richardsons, metal yard in Camberwell, worse than the Krays they were. Got done for armed robbery. Eight years in Parkhurst [prison]. Now I beg. Baker Street, I can get £40 – 50 ($80) in two hours. My wife had a baby with somebody else while I was inside. Three kids. Haven't seen them since 1968. My son is 50. I could be a grandfather. I wouldn't know them. In Becton, being a villain was what you did in them days.' ■

These are the expendables of a society of appearances, the deleted of history – rough sleepers, ragged insomniacs drawn to the gleam of the midnight tea-van; also the unseen, the home-stayers and shut-ins, the frightened agoraphobe and victim of dementia, behind the door barricaded against the terror within, the weak and lonely who hear only voices that echo in their head. They serve their purpose, these furtive lives on the edge of consciousness. Their ill-paid and invisible labor keeps wages low; their threadbare poverty makes their fate a terrible warning and example, calculated to keep everybody else in line.

Life on the margins in the US

In the US, too, poor people have been landscaped out of sight, airbrushed into invisibility by the overwhelming imagery of plenty.

There are an estimated six million undocumented migrants in the US. Farming jobs have created a boom in people-smuggling. According to ABC News, drivers called 'coyotes' sell them to employers. Wages for such work are dropping, but payment to the coyotes is rising. If they can't afford the fee, they pay with their labor. Raids on the fields and farms drive them into the cities, especially in California, New York, Florida, Texas, New Jersey, Illinois and Arizona, where they disperse throughout the low-paid economy, finding work as domestics, in seasonal industries, selling on the streets or laboring.

According to the US Immigration and Naturalization Service, different parts of the country draw migrants from different countries. Overall, the greatest percentage of undocumented migrants comes from Mexico (54 per cent). In California, out of an annual total of some 200,000, it is thought 64,000 are from Mexico, 23,000 from the Philippines and 1,000 from China. In New York, out of about 154,000, there are 25,000 from the former Soviet Union, 21,000 from the Dominican Republic and 11,000 from China. In Florida, out of 79,000, 22,000 are from Cuba, 8,000 from Haiti and 4,000 from Colombia. In New Jersey, out of 63,000, 6,000 are from India, 5,000 from Dominican Republic, 3,000 from Colombia.

The criteria for measuring poverty probably represent a significant undercount. Behind the official

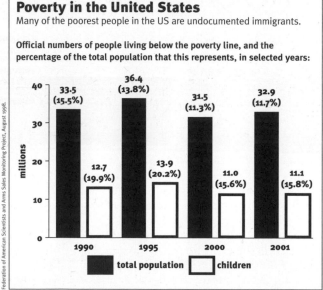

Poverty in the United States

Many of the poorest people in the US are undocumented immigrants.

Official numbers of people living below the poverty line, and the percentage of the total population that this represents, in selected years:

Year	total population	children
1990	33.5 (15.5%)	12.7 (19.9%)
1995	36.4 (13.8%)	13.9 (20.2%)
2000	31.5 (11.3%)	11.0 (15.6%)
2001	32.9 (11.7%)	11.1 (15.8%)

The Arms Trade Revealed, Lora Lumpe and Jeff Donarski, Federation of American Scientists and Arms Sales Monitoring Project, August 1998.

figures an old phenomenon is reappearing – the specter of the laboring poor, as they were called in the early industrial era. These people, no matter how hard they worked, could still not command enough money for the subsistence of themselves and their families.

Poverty USA

US writer Barbara Ehrenreich spent months living in the low-wage economy of America, to see how difficult it was to survive. She worked waitressing, in a care home, marketing and cleaning. She offers great insight into the invisibles, whose labor is unnoticed, who go to and from work at unpredictable hours. At times, she had to take two jobs to make ends meet. Finding affordable accommodation is an heroic undertaking, even trailers and rented rooms proving beyond the means of the low paid. Having paid rent, and waiting for a pay check, she has no money for food. Following labyrinthine inquiries, she learns that food vouchers are available for the working poor. 'My dinner choices... are limited to any two of the following: one box spaghetti noodles, one jar spaghetti sauce, one can of vegetables, one can of baked beans, one pound of hamburger, a box of Hamburger Helper, or a box of Tuna Helper. No fresh fruit or vegetables, no chicken or cheese, and oddly, no tuna to help out with. For breakfast I can have cereal and milk or juice... Bottom line: $7.02 worth of food acquired in 70 minutes of calling and driving, minus $2.80 for the phone calls.'[1]

Ehrenreich also writes of the disappearing poor. Quoting from an article by James Fallows[2] she says of the blindness of the affluent: 'As public [state] schools and other public services deteriorate, those who can afford to do so send their children to private schools and spend their off-hours in private spaces – health clubs, for example, instead of the local park. They don't ride on public buses and subways. They withdraw from mixed neighborhoods into distant suburbs, gated communities or guarded apartment towers; they shop in stores that, in line with the prevailing "market segmentation", are designed to appeal to the affluent alone. Even the affluent young are increasingly unlikely to spend their summers learning how the "other half" lives, as lifeguards, waitresses or housekeepers at resort hotels. *The New York Times* reports that they now prefer career-relevant activities like summer school or interning in an appropriate professional setting to the sweaty, low-paid and mind-numbing slots that have long been their lot.'

Everyone knows unemployment creates poverty. But full employment, too, has the same effect if people are not paid a living wage. Ehrenreich says that in 1999 Massachusetts food pantries reported a 72-per-cent increase in demand for their services over the previous year. The percentage of Wisconsin food-stamp families in 'extreme poverty' – less than 50 per cent of the federal poverty line – has tripled in the last decade.

Anti-poverty agency Bread for the World states that 33 million people – including 13 million children – live in households that experience hunger or the risk of hunger. This represents one in ten households in the US.

In August 2000 19.7 million people participated in the food-stamp program. The US Conference of Mayors reported in 2002 that requests for emergency food assistance increased by an average of 19 per cent. The study found that 48 per cent of those requesting emergency food assistance were members of families with children and that 38 per cent of adults requesting such assistance were employed.

America's Second Harvest, the nation's largest network of food banks, reports that 23.3 million people turned to the agencies they serve in 2001, an increase of over two million since 1997 – 40 per cent were from working families.[3]

Locking the poor away

There is another reason why the poor are incon-
spicuous: so many are locked up. The US presents
the strange paradox of a society which constantly
professes its devotion to freedom in an aggressively
carceral society: a higher percentage of its people is
jailed than in any other country in the world. That
these people are, overwhelmingly, poor and black is
no secret.

Since felons are subsequently disfranchised, the US
now has 1.75 million people disqualified from voting
because of their criminality – 1.4 million black men
have forfeited their right to vote, almost 15 per cent
of the black male population.

Between 1980 and 1996 the US prison population
rose from 1,330,000 to 1,630,940 and by 2005 had
reached 2.1 million, according to the Eisenhower
Foundation. In the years between 1980 and 1996,
prison spending rose from $4 billion to $40 billion.
Including all those passing through the judicial system
at any one time, some four million are caught up in
the mechanisms of justice.

With privatization of the prison system, punishment is a major source of economic growth. What
more effective way of placing the poor out of sight of
respectable citizens? Of course, this is no new thing,
as any student of the Poor Law in Britain will be
aware – incarceration in the workhouse in the 19th
century was also an attempt to compel the persistent
and willful poor to conform to values devised by the
possessing classes.

In the 15 years after 1982, almost 50 new prisons
were built in New York State alone, at a cost of $5
billion. Blacks are almost eight times more likely to be
imprisoned than whites. At 1997 prices, it cost nearly
$150,000 for the construction of each new cell. The
cost of maintaining a prisoner is about $50,000 a
year. In spite of this, 47 per cent of prisoners released

in New York re-offend within a year.[4]

Britain cannot match this level of imprisonment, although in February 2003 it had the distinction in the European Union of overtaking Portugal with the proportion of its population it now locks up, a number in 2005 close to 80,000.

There is another secret about poverty buried in the statistics. Crime has another social role – it represents the privatization of social justice. Collective action for self-improvement has been delegitimized, done away with by official declarations over the death of social-ism. Crime is the response of individuals to socially created wrongs: it is both a caricature of mainstream values (criminals, too, show great enterprise and inge-nuity in their operations), and a celebration of heroic individualism at the heart of capitalism-made-global.

In August 2005, hurricane Katrina, which devas-tated the city of New Orleans, demonstrated to the world the nature of poverty in America. For the waters that swept through the city not only crushed buildings, churches, stores, casinos, factories and clubs, but also deposited a human wreckage on the streets – a used-up humanity, the shut-ins and locked-aways, an incarcerated populace, a secret people, those who pay the true costs of the expensive mainte-nance of the American dream. Most of those unable to flee were the victims of success, the failures, losers of a competitive individualistic society which tries to hide away its hopeless and disappointed in the cellars and attics of forgetting. These people – overwhelm-ingly black – were brutally flushed out by the raging waters. Rarely had they been seen in such multitudes; the concentration of so many infirm and vulnerable, elderly, weak, unhinged and disordered people made visible the ugliness of the social injustice of America.

This event had a global impact. The floating corpses untouched by loving hands, but neglected for days, shocked people in India and Bangladesh, where such calamities are commonplace. In the 1998 monsoon, two-thirds of the landmass of Bangladesh was under water. Fewer people perished than died in New Orleans in 2005. The catastrophe gave the world some insight into the different meaning of poverty between North and South.

Poverty and inequality

Poverty cannot, in any case, easily be separated from social justice. It is one thing to speak of 'meritocratic' societies, whereby people of talent will be rewarded, but the consequences of this for those left behind, contemplating the absence of that merit that earns them a footballer's wage or fat-cat rewards, can be dire. The 'compassion' extended to those left stranded by the onward march of the meritocrats is unlikely to satisfy them.

The American sociologist Richard Sennett states that opportunity and compassion make an unhappy marriage. 'Since Franklin Delano Roosevelt's New Deal, government in America has sought to provide education and work for the ablest poor people. The passion to reward merit persisted even during the dry Reagan years. This strategy largely worked: there are few talented young people who cannot find a good job or a bursary and the welfare state helped build a black petit bourgeoisie.

'But this "creaming" strategy has only increased the gap between the haves and have-nots. The people whom the sociologists call the "unexceptional disadvantaged" have seen their standards of living decline in the past 40 years. Emphasizing social mobility has weakened compassionate care for those left behind.'[5]

The Eisenhower Foundation estimated that real household income in the USA declined by 2.7 per cent between 2000 and 2005. In 2005, the minimum wage was at its lowest level in 56 years. ∎

The invisible poor

As in America, certain emblematic figures appear in the media, often through some sensational event. These become the object of an outpouring of pity and charity, but it is not long before they are swallowed up in the anonymity of statistics and indifference.

Victoria Climbié

In January 2001, Marie-Therese Kouao and Carl Manning were sentenced in London to life imprisonment for the murder of Victoria Climbié, a child of eight.

A relative living in France – a French citizen – visits her relatives near Abidjan in Côte d'Ivoire. She offers to take one of their children to France to give her the opportunity of an education. The parents are happy to entrust their child to one who will promote her chances in life. Who doesn't dream of her child going to the West, becoming a doctor or teacher, returning home to share her prosperity with immediate blood relations and community?

Victoria Climbié left Côte d'Ivoire in 1998 with her great-aunt and went to Paris, where Kouao was living on social security benefit. In Paris, Victoria became the subject of a Child At Risk Emergency Notification when she failed to attend school. Kouao owed money falsely claimed from social security. She took the child and traveled to England, where she told social workers she had come to improve her English for work with an airline.

Within 11 months of arriving in England, Victoria Climbié was dead. She was admitted to hospital in February 2000, her temperature too low to be recorded by a hospital thermometer. She had more than 128 injuries. Although transferred to intensive care she did not survive the day.

Kouao met a bus-driver, Carl Manning, whose bus she boarded one day in July. Within days she and Victoria had moved into his one-room flat. The contact between Kouao (who passed as mother of the child) and four social services departments, two housing departments, the police child-protection service, two hospitals and various evangelical churches – one of which tried to exorcise the 'evil spirits possessing the child' – failed to rescue Victoria from her tormentors. Directly or indirectly, they encountered some 150 functionaries of the caring society.

Victoria was rarely spoken to by social workers, who regarded the mother as their 'client.' Victoria was virtually invisible. All that remained of her was the memory of a dazzling smile and, of course, the appalling injuries she sustained.

She remained 'unseen' by those paid to protect her. During the 305 days she spent in Britain, she was never enrolled in any school. ■

Marginalizing the world's poor people

When domestic poverty in the rich world has been effectively concealed, it is easy to avoid the global issue. After all, the places visited by the rich appear principally in glossy brochures and holiday publicity; travelers look for unspoilt beaches, breathtaking scenery where smiling waiters serve at limpid poolsides and exotically costumed locals perform traditional dances for the entertainment of guests.

A distinction might be made between travel and tourism – the mirror-image of the travels of desperation which take the poor to the sites of imagined plenty. The world which the rich make their playground is crafted to be picturesque and scenic; even some of the poorest countries now promote themselves as tourist destinations. The Gambia, Tanzania, South Africa and Kenya are promoted for their clear waters, dramatic wildlife and stunning scenery. These are also places where millions are dying of AIDS, where violent crime is commonplace and pitiless social injustice prevails. But this does not impinge upon the enjoyments which the well-to-do purchase for themselves.

When the poverty of the world appears in the hectic media schedules of the rich, it does so as an appeal to their charitable instincts, to write a check, to sponsor a child, to make a life better. The appeal to a genuine and heartfelt altruism dissolves into the exaltations of sentimentality – the fundamental relationships between privilege and poverty remain unchanged.

Occasionally worlds collide: an asylum-seeker is knifed to death on the streets of Glasgow; a hostel for migrants is set on fire in Frankfurt; a Moroccan is shot by an angry occupant of a public-housing scheme in Creteil in France. Sometimes, those who have been sent in search of a better life discover they have an appointment, not with improvement, but with death.

The invisible poor

Preserving the poor

It is now taken for granted that relief of poverty is the chief objective of all politicians, international institutions, donors and charities. This dedication is revealed most clearly in a determination to preserve them. Like all great historical monuments, there should be a Society for the Preservation of the Poor; only, since that is written into the very structures of the global economy, no special arrangements are required. There is not the remotest chance that poverty will be abolished, but every chance that the poor themselves might perish.

Poverty line

In Britain the poverty line is set at 60 per cent of median income. As rich people become much richer, the median rises and more people apparently become poor.[5] This definition ensures poverty a kind of immortality. It is an admission that poverty is built into the model of constant growth. As a result, there is no prospect that those living off poor people are going to lose their livelihood. The poor are treated as though they were an inert mass, waiting to be lifted out of poverty by the buoyancy of the economy, the rising tide of affluence. They will – at least since the official funeral orations over the death of socialism – not be the agents of their own deliverance. They are objects of development.

If they do anything collectively, they immediately coalesce into 'mobs', creating 'disturbances' to civil order, throwing stones, bombs or worse. They remain deserving only when they appear as the focus of the noble endeavors of others, well-to-do others, of course.

Poor people do not speak for themselves. The mute button has been pushed on the global, as well as the domestic, poor. Hands reach out in entreaty after a disaster, homes wrecked by a cyclone, civil strife, environmental ruin, a face contorted with pain, a belly swollen with hunger. These images tell no story: a CNN or BBC commentator is always at hand to inform. 'These people have lost everything.' 'These people have nowhere to go.' 'These people are on the edge of survival.'

These people. Voiceless, apparently struck dumb by their poverty, they have been forced into a vow of silence; because, of course, they have nothing to say.

What story might such people tell, should they speak? There is a very good reason for the ventriloqual interpretations of poverty by the spokespersons of wealth. For the voice of poor people asks only for security, sufficiency, an assurance that they will be granted enough for their needs, space to bring up a new generation, not in luxury but in peace and an absence of want.

And these are what they cannot have. The dynamic of wealth creation depends crucially upon insecurity, the limitlessness of satisfaction – economic growth. Images of the wretched, famished and entreating serve to goad the entrepreneurs and go-getters, the hard-working and the devotees of wealth creation, to even greater feats of economic prowess. Without the image of poverty, who would submit to the stress, violence and excesses which drive us on, constantly in fear that we might sink back into the mass of what are sometimes brutally referred to as the 'have-nots?'

It is not that poverty is 'incurable', like some genetically determined disease. It is the very modesty of the demands of the poor that drowns out their voices in the incoherent concert of the global media.

They are indeed a danger to wealth, but not quite in the way they are represented to be. It is the simplicity of their wishes that determines that they should be gagged; precisely because the necessities are readily available, but they must remain deprived, for reasons that are wholly ideological and have nothing to do with scarcity.

The invisible poor

To lift up poor people requires, not more growth, but a more rigorous evaluation of what constitutes wealth – and the poverties it engenders. It demands something more than the hyperactivity of the artful business of false devotion to poverty alleviation.

1 Barbara Ehrenreich, *Nickel and Dimed*, Henry Holt, New York, 2001. **2** *New York Times Magazine*, 19 March 2000. **3** www.bread.org/hungerbasics/domestic.html **4** Sasha Abramsky, *Toward Freedom*, May 1997. **5** *The Guardian*, 17 June 2002.

2 Measuring poverty

There's no shortage of facts and figures, or of different ways to interpret them. The measures are crude; the pathways for climbing out of poverty impossible for the majority to follow. The question is: if the world has got so much richer, why has poverty not disappeared?

'Give me neither riches nor poverty, but enough for my sustenance.'
Book of Isaiah.

A FOLK-TALE, common to many cultures in Asia and Africa, challenges the wisdom of getting rich. It goes like this:

> A traveler observes a fisherman sleeping in the shade of a tree. He rouses the sleeping man and asks him why he isn't catching fish. 'I already caught two fish for my family's evening meal.' 'If you had a bigger net and worked longer, you could catch ten fish,' says the stranger. 'But I only need two. What would I do with ten?' 'You could sell them. Do the same every day until you have enough money to buy a boat.' 'Why would I do that?' 'To catch even more fish. You could employ people, and send them out to catch more. You would grow rich.' 'What would I do with the money?' 'You could enjoy yourself. You could relax, sit and enjoy yourself and go to sleep in the shade.' 'What am I doing now?' asks the fisherman.

Who needs to learn about poverty? Most people on earth have long been familiar with it; many are terrified that it might claim them once more; the rest have run as far away from it as they can.

Statistics are published and republished. Every aid agency, international institution, humanitarian organization spreads awareness of the facts. The question of why these facts have made so little impact upon the growing injustice in the world is central to this book.

All the statistics on poverty – often conflicting, but asserted as though they were holy writ – should be regarded with caution. Many, especially those gathered by poor countries with few facilities for accurate measurement, are unreliable at best, and sometimes glaringly fictitious. For these are almost invariably published by governments or institutions which have a vested interest in proving to the world that we are making 'progress'. The World Bank claims that 'extreme poverty' fell from 28 per cent in 1990 to 19 per cent in 2002 should be regarded with skepticism: it seems that the more remote from the experience of poor people institutions become, the greater the authority with which they judge them.

Inequality

There are other ways of looking at poverty. One is the growth over time of inequality, both between and within countries. It is important to distinguish between poverty and inequality, for the former measures a state of absolute want (absence of necessities indispensable for survival) and the latter is an index of social injustice. Poverty may be reduced while inequality increases.

Whichever way you look at it, extreme poverty persists while social injustice increases all the time. This has a powerful impact on discussions of poverty, since the model of improvement embodied in globalization is that *the poor will become a little less poor only if the rich become much richer.*

Almost one in five people in all the developing countries are not expected to survive beyond 40. Sierra Leone has the lowest life expectancy in the world – about 38, less than half that of Japan, which has reached 80. While 20 per cent of children born in the

Source: UN statistics

Snapshots

The numbers of people living in poverty are well known, although the figures conceal as much as they tell.

- More than 840 million people in the world are malnourished
- Six million children under the age of five die every year as a consequence of malnutrition
- 1.2 billion people in the world live on less than a dollar a day. Half the world's people live on less than two dollars a day
- The income of the richest 1% of people in the world is equal to that of the poorest 57%
- In the developing world, 91 children out of every 1,000 die before their fifth birthday
- 12 million people die annually from lack of water; 1.1. billion do not have access to clean water; 2.4 billion live without proper sanitation
- 40 million people are living with AIDS
- More than 113 million children in the developing world have no basic education; 60% of them are girls
- Women are still the poorest of the poor, representing 70% of those in absolute poverty
- Women work two-thirds of the world's working hours, produce half the world's food, yet earn only 10% of the world's income and own less than 1% of the world's property. ■

poorest countries will still die before the age of five, in the richest countries less than one per cent will do so.

Increasing longevity in industrialized countries was due to a remarkable improvement in public and environmental health, particularly in sanitation and the quality of water. This, combined with rising living standards, better nutrition and housing, created new patterns of disease in the rich world, a shift from infectious and waterborne sickness to chronic disorders like heart disease and cancer. There are signs that among the privileged of the South today a similar transition is occurring, although the poorest remain prey to patterns of disease that were common in Britain in the early 19th century.

Growing life expectancy and declining child mortality in the South are only in small measure due to improved sanitation (since 2.8 billion people in the world exist with no satisfactory waste-disposal system), and owe more to the availability of cheap drugs, especially antibiotics and rehydration therapies.

It should, perhaps, not be taken for granted that the pathway to 'development' of the West can be replicated throughout the world: the vast public expenditure that created the health infrastructure of the rich world is unlikely to be available to the Governments of India, China, Brazil or Indonesia for the foreseeable future.

The bottom 20

The World Bank has refined its judgment of the world's poorest countries. It now makes a distinction between per-capita income (which it now calls Gross National Income, or GNI) and its purchasing power parity (PPP). This latter measure gives an indication of what this income will actually buy, in terms of US dollars.

The difference between Gross National Income (GNI) and Purchasing Power Parity (PPP) of the world's poorest countries.

Country	GNI per capita ($)	Position	PPP	Position
Ethiopia	100	1	710	7
Burundi	100	2	590	4
Sierra Leone	140	3	480	1
Guinea-Bissau	160	4	710	6
Tajikistan	170	5	1,150	21
Niger	170	6	770	9
Malawi	170	7	620	5
Eritrea	190	8	970	15
Chad	200	9	930	14
Mozambique	210	10	1,000	17
Mali	210	11	810	11
Burkina Faso	210	12	1,020	19
Rwanda	220	13	1,000	16
Nepal	250	14	1,450	26
Madagascar	260	15	870	13
Togo	270	16	1,420	25
Tanzania	270	17	540	2
Cen African Rep	270	18	1,180	22
Cambodia	270	19	1,520	29

Afghanistan is also among the poorest, but data are not available.

Source: World Bank World Development Report 2001 www.worldbank.org

Climbing out of poverty

It has been assumed that most countries in the world will become rich in the same way as the West did, adopting Western patterns of wealth-creation. Recently, however – especially given the vast increase in global wealth – the question has been posed why certain countries and regions of the world are failing to reduce the numbers of people in absolute poverty.

According to the United Nations Commission on Trade and Development (UNCTAD): 'The inadequacy of the analytical foundations for effective poverty reduction in poor countries in general, and in the least developed countries in particular, is not generally recognized.'[1]

This may come as a surprise, considering that the condition of the poor has been a major preoccupation of policy-makers ever since the Industrial Revolution two centuries ago. We might expect some radical new understanding in this UNCTAD report which claims to show the way forward for the Poverty Reduction Strategies to which the 'international community' has committed itself. It turns out to be lacking both in blinding insights and in new departures. 'Its central message is that there is a major, but currently underestimated, opportunity for rapid reduction

---

The great divide

- The assets of the 200 richest people in the world are worth more than the total annual income of 41% of the world's people
- Three families – Bill Gates, the Sultan of Brunei and the Walton family (Wal-Mart) – have a combined wealth of some $135 billion. This equals the annual income of 600 million people living in the world's poorest countries
- The UN Human Development Index states that the richest 20% of the world's population receive 150 times the wealth of the poorest 20%. In 1960, the share of the global income of the bottom 20% was 2.3%. By 1991, this had fallen to 1.4%. ■

UNDP *Human Development Report* 1997, 1998, 1999;
World Development Movement 1999.

in extreme poverty in the LDCs [Least Developed Countries] through sustained economic growth.'

The report states that over one billion people live in countries whose governments are preparing Poverty Reduction Strategy papers, as a condition for

---

Identifying poverty

Some commonly used measures:

Consumption
- The richest fifth of the world's people consume 45% of the world's meat and fish; the poorest fifth 5%
- The richest fifth consume 58% of total energy, the poorest fifth less than 4%
- The richest fifth have 74% of all telephone lines, the poorest fifth 1.5%
- The richest fifth use 84% of all paper, the poorest 20 per cent 1.1%
- The richest fifth own 87% of the world's vehicles, the poorest fifth less than 1%.

Literacy
- There are today about one billion non-literate adults; two-thirds of them are women, of whom 98% live in developing countries
- 52% of non-literates live in India and China
- In sub-Saharan Africa, primary school enrollment has declined from 58% to 50% since 1980
- In the least developed countries 45% of children do not attend school
- Per-capita income in countries with a literacy rate of less than 55% averages about $600
- In countries with a literacy rate between 55% and 84% income averages $2,400
- Where the literacy rate is between 85% and 95% income reaches $3,700
- Countries with a literacy rate above 96% have an income of $12,600

Life expectancy
- In the richest countries, average life expectancy climbed from about 67 years in 1950 to 77 in 1995
- In the developing countries it grew from 40 to 64 years
- In the least developed countries it has increased from 36 to 52 years, although in large parts of Africa it is falling once more as a result of HIV/AIDS
- In 1950 287 children in every 1,000 born in the developing world would die before reaching the age of five. By 1995 this had dropped to 90. ■

Source: UNICEF, *State of the World's Children*, UNESCO, UN statistics

access to concessional aid and debt relief. It goes on to describe 'an alternative approach to the design of poverty reduction strategies, which will double average household living standards through growth-oriented macroeconomic policies, the building of domestic productive capacities and strategic integration into the global economy...' In other words, the only prescription for poverty reduction in the world remains unchanged – economic growth.

Least developed countries

Many countries of the developing world still bear the scars of an imperialist past, in the sense that they still depend disproportionately upon the supply of raw materials to the rich world.

According to UN statistics, the 49 'least developed countries' depend upon agriculture and fishing for more than 36 per cent of their gross domestic product, and 80 per cent of their export revenues. These countries are not the same as those with the lowest per-capita income. They 'suffer from long-term handicaps to growth, in particular, low levels of human resource development and/or severe structural weaknesses'. According to the UN, 'the group represents the weakest segment of humanity and presents a major challenge to its development partners'.

The criteria for LDC status are: a low-income criterion (below $900 per capita); a human-weakness criterion, based on indicators of nutrition, health, education and adult literacy; and an economic criterion, based on indicators of instability of agricultural production; instability of exports of goods and services; the economic importance of non-traditional activities (share of manufacturing and modern services in GDP); merchandise export concentration; the handicap of economic smallness.

Of these countries, 30 are in Africa, 13 in the Asia-Pacific region, 5 are Arab States, and 1 is in the

Least developed countries

These are the countries which the UN believes, by a variety of measures, have the most 'development' still to do.

Afghanistan	Eritrea	Nepal
Angola	Ethiopia	Niger
Bangladesh	Gambia	Rwanda
Benin	Guinea	São Tomé & Principé
Bhutan	Guinea-Bissau	Senegal
Burkina Faso	Haiti	Sierra Leone
Burundi	Kiribati	Solomon Islands
Cambodia	Laos	Somalia
Cape Verde	Lesotho	Sudan
Central African	Liberia	Tanzania
Republic	Madagascar	Togo
Chad	Malawi	Tuvalu
Comoros	Maldives	Uganda
Democratic Republic	Mali	Vanuatu
of Congo	Mauritania	Western Samoa
Djibouti	Mozambique	Yemen
Equatorial Guinea	Myanmar (Burma)	Zambia

Source: UN

Americas. The most populous is Bangladesh, with 147 million people.

Many of these countries are currently losing market shares in their principal exports. They have become net commodity importers, with combined exports in the sector of $6.8 billion annually, against $9.0 billion in imports. They are also net importers of food: their total annual exports in the sector, taking account of coffee, tobacco, tea and cocoa, reached $3.8 billion, but their imports for the same period exceeded $7.9 billion.[2]

In 2005, the World Trade Organization reported that the rise in oil prices dramatically advantaged certain countries. Major suppliers of fuels and mining products increased their exports by one-third in dollar terms. The chief beneficiaries of this were the Russian Federation, Saudi Arabia, Iran, Venezuela, Algeria, Kuwait and Nigeria. In the same year, the US trade deficit rose to $793 billion, and China's trade surplus (2006 figures) reached $177.47 billion.

Growth of world trade

According to the World Trade Organization, during the 50 years of the General Agreement on Tariffs and Trade (GATT – out of which the World Trade Organization grew):

- Global merchandise trade grew annually by 6%, or 18-fold.
- Output of merchandise grew by 4.2% annually, or 8-fold.
- The share of world Gross Domestic Product (GDP) represented by merchandise trade grew from under 7% to 17.4%.
- Aggregate world trade in 1998 was $6.6 trillion, of which $5.3 trillion (80%) was merchandise and $1.3 trillion (20%) was commercial services.
- GDP per capita grew by 1.9% annually.
- On average, per-capita income was 2.5 times higher in 1998 than it was in 1948.

Developed countries, especially those of the European Union (EU), have increased their share of world commodity exports, principally as a result of their domestic agricultural-support policies. Between the early 1970s and the late 1990s industrialized countries saw their share of commodity exports rise from 58.8 per cent to 66.3 per cent, the EU increasing from 28.2 per cent to 38.6 per cent. By contrast, developing countries held a share of 31.5 per cent of world commodities in the early 1970s; by the late 1990s, this had fallen to 26.3 per cent.

The share in world trade of sub-Saharan Africa remained unchanged between 1998 and 2004, at 1.5 per cent. The World Bank reports however that primary products, as a percentage of exports, decreased from 88 per cent in 1998 to 73 per cent in 2004. The Bank states that specific products have lessened the dependency on primary commodities, citing cut flowers from Rwanda, music from Mali and clothing and textiles from Mauritius, Lesotho and Madagascar.

Loss of market share by the poorest countries is only partly accounted for by the continuing downward trend in the prices of traditional commodities like coffee, cocoa, sugar and cotton; subsidies to the farmers of

---

Trade talks

In July 2006, the Doha Round negotiations of the World Trade Organization collapsed. This round of negotiations, which began in 2001, was to have been a 'development round'. Nothing could have been further from the truth. While demanding that poor countries reduce their tariffs on agricultural and industrial goods from the rich world and at the same time open up to Western financial, insurance and other service sectors, the US insisted on maintaining agricultural subsidies worth $20 billion, while Europe, although phasing out direct agricultural subsidies, would have kept 55 billion euros' worth in other forms of export support. Development economist Walden Bello, of Focus on the Global South, stated that the collapse of Doha is the best outcome for developing countries. He says: 'Not only do the economic costs of a potential Doha conclusion clearly outweigh any projected benefits to the poor; the loss of policy space for developing countries – to create jobs through industrialization, guarantee public services and protect farmers and food security – would be tantamount to kicking away the ladder of development, and prevent developing nations from using the very tools used by developed nations to pull themselves out of poverty.' ■

Walden Bello, Focus on the Global South, July 25, 2006 www.focusweb.org/

Source: UN statistics

---

the rich world are also a major determinant.

When the global institutions want to spread the word of their success, they produce some astonishing figures.

The question is, how can poverty possibly survive such stupendous increases in wealth and trade? If the creation of wealth really were the answer, poverty would have been conquered long ago. Yet half the world still lives on less than two dollars a day. This contradiction requires a closer scrutiny than it has, perhaps, until now received.

1 UNCTAD/LDC/2002/Overview 2 Gustavo Capdevila, *Commodities*, Third World Network. www.twnside.org.sg.

3 Defining poverty

How ideas about poverty assume limitless economic growth – and limitless desires. Absolute and relative poverty – the colonialism of development, the colonization of sufficiency and the poverty of wealth.

A population expert complains that a village family is poor because there are too many children. The mother angrily lines up her twelve children outside the hut, and says to him: 'Now, look at them, and tell me which ones I should not have had.'

IT MAY SEEM that poverty requires no definition. Everyone recognizes 'the poor' who appear daily on the TV screens of the world. Who is unfamiliar with images of children and old people, haggard and exhausted, fleeing the war-zone in central Africa or the cyclone in Southeast Asia, the drought-stricken areas of Zimbabwe or Ethiopia; the distended stomach and discolored hair of malnourishment, the skeletal figures lying listlessly while the flies encrust their eyes?
This is the 'absolute poverty' of those who have nothing, people whose lives are in constant danger from the lack of basic resources for survival.

Poverty stares us in the face. It is, in one way, the constant companion of all of us. Its presence, or rather the symbols of its presence, serve a number of purposes.

It inspires people to acts of charity – whether because their hearts are touched by privation in a world of plenty or a superstitious warding off of the specter. People do give, although charity can at best only alleviate the very worst examples and offer temporary relief to those overtaken by disaster.

These images of humanity on the edge of existence also serve as a terrible warning: look, they say, to what depths you might fall, if you cease to work and to strive. They are a deterrent: no-one is ignorant of the fate of the poor. This spurs people to greater economic effort, particularly when all that stands between us and the condition of the poorest is the labor of our hands or the ingenuity of our brains.

This poverty is the concern of aid agencies, governments and international financial institutions. Given the resolve of the most powerful on earth, surely it cannot be long before such relentless want is answered and these scenes cease to haunt the world. That this has not yet already happened remains one of the puzzles of the age: with such commitment to poverty abatement by the wealthy, how can such wretchedness persist?

Hunger

Hunger and the threat of famine are the most potent symbols of poverty. The periodic appearance of starvation in a world which can bring television soap operas and Coca-Cola to the remotest places on earth is the most damaging indictment of a system which sets wealth creation above everything.

There is enough food in the world to provide every human being with 3,500 calories a day. Scarcity is not the problem, but the absence of purchasing power of the ill-nourished to buy in the market. It is a lack of distributive justice which leaves at least 800 million hungry and, in 2003, threatened wide-scale famine in Southern and East Africa.[1]

It is almost impossible to describe constant hunger to those who have never felt it.

Not long ago, even in the West, hunger was ever-present. My grandmother used to put her children to bed in the afternoon, with sacks at the windows so they would believe it was night and not feel hunger. An old woman told me that during a strike in the leather factories in 1895 she collected snails from the damp places behind brick walls, soaked them in salt

Farida Bibi

Here is Farida Bibi in a village near Barisal on the Bay of Bengal, a landless woman with three children, whose only resource is seasonal wage-labor:

'In the morning, we eat a little rice diluted with water. At midday we are given bread by people in whose fields we work. In the evening we eat rice and vegetables. In the lean season, we eat only rotis with chilli and salt to give it some taste.

'You dream of food all the time. You fear the mornings, because you will wake up hungry and hear the children crying. I have picked up sugarcane that other people have eaten and thrown away to give them something to chew. We have cooked leaves from trees and roots from the earth. When you have no land and no money to buy in the market, you do not go near it: it is torture to see what you cannot have.

'Hunger moves inside you like a living thing. At first it makes you restless, but then you grow tired. You don't waste energy by moving about. Sleep is your only escape. You lose interest in the world, hunger eats your flesh. To feed the children is your only concern. You work for neighbors in exchange for a little rice or vegetable. You become small. You lose appetite. Then the thought of food stops being a dream. It frightens you. You wonder how you managed to eat. You lose your relationship to food; you lose all relationship with your own body.

'We have chewed rags. I sent my daughter to the town to live as a maidservant. She is ten. I do not have to find food for her. When she comes home she brings something from the table of her employers. That is a feast day.' ∎

for 24 hours and boiled them. Such efforts are familiar today in most countries where there is food scarcity. Traditional cultures knew of reserves of 'famine foods' – fruits, tubers, wild vegetables; many of these have been used up, as familiar environments have been transformed, forests felled, landscapes destroyed.

An important milestone was reached in 2006. US Professor Barry Popkin of the University of North Carolina told the International Association of Agricultural Economists that the number of overweight people in the world was now greater than the number of malnourished. Obesity has overtaken hunger: more than one billion people are overweight, while 820 million are underfed. It is difficult to imagine a more telling statistic to illustrate the imbalance in the world economy. Excess and insufficiency are part and parcel of the same global system.

Being alone

A woman in her sixties in Tanzania said: 'You are poor when you have seen your seven children die of AIDS. When the people you expect to take care of you in old age die before you, who will you turn to?'

In some parts of South and East Africa, a generation of young adults has been decimated by AIDS. Elderly women remain to look after orphans, some of whom are themselves HIV-positive. This is against the natural order. 'There is nothing worse than to see your children die, when you have brought them safely through childhood. That is why we have children. They owe you their survival, and they will save you from want in old age.'

Much discussion of poverty and population ignores the evidence of the rich countries. What makes people limit their families is not 'education' or 'birth control', certainly not 'self-restraint': it is security. When people know they will be cared for as they grow older, families grow smaller. This happened in the West. The children of the poor represent a future free from need. Security is what people want, not contraceptives, programs of sterilization or advice on sexual abstinence.

The villages of Tanzania, Malawi, South Africa are haunted by the ghosts of those who did not live out their lives. Dirt mounds mark the graves, not only of children who died of avoidable diseases, but of adults who perished in their prime, human sacrifice to a global market which failed to provide them with medicines to prolong their days.

The only resource of most people in the world against poverty is not a 'safety-net' of welfare payments, but networks of flesh and blood, kin and family. These provide their only protection – shelter, food and nursing for the sick and aged. 'Development' erodes these provisions – through urbanization, migration, the break-up of families, as people travel in search of livelihood. The South is the site of a vast, untried experiment: what will happen as old forms of security decay and governments cannot afford a financial substitute?

Rural poor people

According to a report from the UN International Fund for Agricultural Development (IFAD), three quarters of the poorest people in the world live in rural areas.

Rural poverty, however, cannot be dissociated from urbanization and industrialization. Few rural households remain untouched, directly or indirectly, by industrial society. Growing dependency upon 'inputs', high-yielding seeds, fertilizer, pesticides, have changed farms and villages from independent rural communities into outposts of a global industrial economy.

Urban populations must be fed, and since these are highly concentrated and liable to react violently if they go hungry, the scattered, docile peasants, the food producers, have been systematically cheated.

Too little – and too much

Poverty and wealth, scarcity and surfeit, are linked together. Every year, lives are lost or shortened by both. Here's one attempt to measure how much life is lost, and to which cause.

Attributable years of life lost by risk factor (world, millions, 2000):

Underweight	127
Unsafe sex	76
Unsafe water & sanitation	49
Tobacco	46
Cholesterol	35
Iron deficiency	26
Overweight	23
Urban air pollution	6

Source: World Health Organization, *World Health Report 2002* www.who.int

---

The prawn farmers

Sathkira, near the Sunderbans, in Bangladesh. Prawnfields close to the coast have flooded paddy-fields with salt water, leaving them grey and desolate. Rice farmers have become laborers in the prawnfields. Traditional shrimp-gatherers who trailed their hand-held nets along the mangrove swamps have lost their livelihood, since the small fry have been taken to stock industrial ponds; their catch has dwindled to almost nothing.

Mumtaz, Shajeda and Fatima stand in the water 12 hours a day. Before the prawn industry killed the mangroves, they earned 100 taka ($2) a day. Now they are lucky to make 20 or 30. None of the women has land. Fatima's husband died 15 years ago, and she stays on land belonging to her family. Mumtaz, abandoned by her husband, lives in a shelter by the roadside. Shajeda lives in her grandfather's homestead.

Jehanara and Anchara are also working. They do not know their age, but are probably 10 or 11. Their heads hang like dark flowers, their arms delicate as young bamboo.

Here, economic violence becomes visible, brutal as a wound in the flesh. The sustaining environment turns against them: what was benign has been made hostile by others. In their debilitated, wasted bodies you can also see the forces at work that evict people from the rural economy. They will soon migrate, rent a house in a slum in Khulna, become domestic servants. ■

This is the most common form of subsidy to urban consumers. This cheating is so systematic that growing food – the most vital of human undertakings – has become stigmatized. Young people, especially those with some education, leave the rural areas – they will not work in the fields. Agricultural work is beneath their dignity.

It is a savage irony that migrants say that in the city they can at least eat. People go hungry in the places where food crops are cultivated. In urban areas that are given priority in the 'modern' economy, the opportunities for work enable them to buy the necessities for survival.

Although the rural poor depend heavily upon agriculture, public spending and international aid support to agriculture fell by two-thirds between 1987 and 1998.[2] The staple food – rice, maize, wheat

– provides 70 to 80 per cent of the calories that people living in rural poverty require. Such is the situation that the IFAD report admits that in some countries there are too many 'deeply poor' to be affected even by the universal panacea of economic growth.

Even in 'remote' areas, global forces drive the poor out of traditional livelihoods.

In Bangladesh, almost 80 per cent of people work in agriculture but own only 5 per cent of the country's resources. Landlessness has increased from 31 per cent of the population at Independence in 1971 to 67 per cent now – a vast-scale alienation of land from small farmers.

This is not going to be reversed by all the top-down

Ghugudah Bheel

The story of Ghugudah Bheel in North Bangladesh is famous: 1,700 acres of *khas* (government-owned) land designated for redistribution for the poor was occupied by rich landlords. It was taken back and redistributed to the Landless Welfare Society, supported by Samata, a non-government organization formed by a group of young people in 1976.

Ghugudah Bheel is a water-body which provided fish, the main source of protein to the poor. It became khas land when the *zamindari* system (the British colonial landlord system) was abolished in 1954. The water was drained and 3,000 acres were seized by former zamindars. Local poor people were offered deeds to land if they gave free labor to clear and prepare it for cultivation. They were then given false papers, to pay for which they had to go into debt.

'Before we organized,' says Sekander Ali, 'it was a tragic life. We were day-laborers and fishing-people, and we migrated seasonally to Rajshahi. There we worked, often for no money, just food twice a day. Women worked for 500 grams of rice of the poorest quality.'

When Samata first took over land the landlords filed false cases against them in the court, accusing them of murder, robbery and rape. Many were imprisoned. The landlords bribed police, judges, politicians. By the persistence of Samata, land was eventually assigned to the landless. Many now have three *bighas* (half a hectare), which has transformed their lives.

As their power declined many landowners moved to Dhaka, where they own real estate, factories and construction companies. Their stranglehold over the rural poor has been weakened. Their field of operations has moved to the cities. ■

agencies which have declared poverty-alleviation as their principal purpose. It can be addressed only by popular action.

Leaving it behind

The passage from absolute poverty is not a simple journey. Most poor people experience times of plenty. When there is demand for labor, at harvest-time, during the rains, when homestead vegetables are ready, people have periods of sufficiency. In many countries rural people take the number of months with enough food as a measure of poverty. To have three months of sufficiency is to be very poor, nine months far less so.

A critical factor in poverty is not only intensity of want but also duration. Nowhere in the world do poor people say they long for economic growth. They want security: to raise a new generation free from hunger, thirst and exposure to sun, rain or cold. Security, however, remains elusive, even for the well-off. In the rich countries people live in fear that their livelihood might be terminated. They dread being declared redundant, superfluous to requirements.

For the poor, loss of livelihood is more dire. The balance between hunger and sufficiency is delicate.

In the city, too, people live for daily survival. It is impossible to plan. A woman in Dar es Salaam, Tanzania, said: 'Poor people have no future. They have only today, and the days they have passed.'

A woman in the Himalayan foothills speaks of the death of her buffalo:

'It was the saddest day of my life. Like losing a child. The animal was pregnant. She gave milk for the children, with some to sell in the market. She pulled the plow. She lived inside our house. We loved her and the smell of her breath. We used the dung for fuel. Then she stopped eating. The baby died inside her. The night she died, we sat with her, and our hearts were sad. We have lost more than we can say. My husband has gone away to find work, but all he knows is working in our field.' ■

Luisa

Evening in the *favela*. This is São Paulo, but it could be Nairobi, Manila or Mexico City. Crowds of workers streaming home in the dusk. Through chinks in the tin and plywood of the huts lights – kerosene or illegal electric connections – throw shadows on the stony ground, glinting on the waste water that trickles through the crooked streets. In a clearing vendors sit with their little heaps of vegetables – red carrots, pale onions, specked cauliflowers, purple eggplants. People are buying for the evening meal. Luisa watches with her two boys aged six and eight. As soon as she sees her husband's familiar figure she sends the children to meet him. His clothes are stained with cement, he carries a plastic bag with his construction tools. When he sees the children his tired face is transformed. He puts down his bag. The younger one jumps onto his shoulder, the other takes his hand and picks up the toolkit. Luisa breathes a sigh of relief. They will eat this evening. Every day anxiety nags her: there are so many accidents on construction sites, there is no certainty there will be work tomorrow. He gives her his money. In every hut the cooking fires with their bright orange flames and gray smoke are little bonfires of celebration: they have come safely through another day. ■

People in poverty are not a static group. They fall into poverty and rise out of it, not only with the season but also with the changing times of life. They are poor as children. As young adults they become less poor. When they start their own family they fall into poverty again. When the children grow up, times are easier. In old age they become poor once more.

People find work and lose it again. Some migrate to another town or are recruited for work abroad. Whole villages in Java, Korat and Luzon are sustained by remittances from domestic workers in the Gulf, sex workers in Bangkok, factory workers in Manila and Dhaka, nurses and au pairs in Europe.

The city provides spaces in which the ingenuity of the poor can find expression.

Relative poverty

For many – perhaps most – people, poverty is relative. That is to say, we compare ourselves to those around us, particularly people better off than we are. This cuts us even more keenly than pictures of misery conveyed by the electronic media. We look to near-equals and wonder whether or not they have a better deal than we do.

Immediate comparisons have great power: they urge us into a competitive struggle with neighbors and acquaintances. The strongest stimulus to our sense of social justice appears to be when we feel our own worth unrecognized. Why should I, as a nurse or firefighter, be worse off than a teacher or a builder? is a characteristic question. Who 'deserves' more than I do?

This familiar touchstone of relative deprivation is sometimes described in Britain as 'keeping up with the Joneses' – a mythical family representing those whose living standards are a little above our own. The question, who are the Joneses trying to keep up with? is not part of the discussion. It should be, since this homely family image is also the justification for a striving which bears little relation to human need, and every relation to economic necessity. Does the economy serve human beings, or has humanity been pressed into the service of the economy?

Howrah Station

A vast imperial structure beside the Hoogly River in Kolkata. Many children live here among the crowds – runaways, orphans, abandoned children. They survive on money from travelers and ride the trains across India, unchallenged, ticketless, earning a few rupees by sweeping the carriages.

A group of boys aged between about 8 and 14 wait for the train to come in. As soon as the people get off they jump onto the train, pick up the empty mineral-water bottles. They sell them for half a rupee (one US cent) each. The middleman cleans them at the drinking fountain, fills them with water from the public tap and then sells them to the stallholders for five or six rupees each. The stallholder 're-seals' the plastic top of the bottle with a candle-flame which slightly melts the plastic. He sells them to the public for 10 or 12 rupees. One boy says: 'We don't need education for our life, we need to be smart.' ∎

Imran Ahmed Siddiqui, *The Statesman*, Kolkata, 2003
www.thestatesman.net

The poverty of the rich

There is another poverty, which afflicts the well-off. Rich people often complain of the things they cannot afford – another holiday, a second home, a new swimming pool. A subjective sense of deprivation affects almost everyone in the rich Western societies. And this gives us a clue as to who the Joneses are trying to keep up with. It has nothing to do with status-seeking or the possessions or lifestyle of others; it has to do with the virtually limitless capacity of the global economy to produce. The gross annual product of the world economy was over $60 trillion in 2006. In the presence of the abundance of the global hypermarket, everyone is bound to feel poor.

Human aspirations are infinite. They always have been. We long for the impossible. Who would not wish for immortality and omnipotence, if these were available? Perhaps the strongest appeal of continuous economic growth is its claim to cater to the limitlessness of human desire. The contradiction between human desire and the circumstances of our brief, fragile lives has been the object of the great religious teachings of the ages. Self-restraint, modest resource use, frugality, non-attachment to material things have been regarded as the beginnings of wisdom. That they have often been exploited for the social control of people does not invalidate them. Of course, the poor have always been told they should lay up treasures in heaven, concern themselves with their immortal soul rather than with the needs of the day. But the abuse of religion for other ends (the self-protection of castes of priests, rulers and powerful élites) should not be confused with the spiritual needs of humanity, which are as basic as the need for food and water.

Doctrines of thrift and austerity have been swept away. Consumerism has harnessed ancient (and unrealizable) human yearnings to a social and economic system which has pretensions, if not to answer them, at least to provide people with consolations for its inability to do so. How unlike traditional religions, which have promised people rewards in paradise or in an afterlife. Global capitalism says you can have it all in the here and now; and this is irresistible to a poor, wanting humanity.

The problem is that as wealth grows so, too, does poverty. The great truth that poverty stunts and diminishes humanity conceals an even greater lie: that human life is enhanced in direct proportion to the amount of wealth an individual enjoys. The opposite of poverty is not wealth, but sufficiency. Satisfaction, contentment, enough for a secure sustenance are what the poor want. Instead they are offered the pursuit of riches. This by-passes sufficiency and makes satisfaction more and more elusive.

This is why definitions of poverty are so difficult. In political and economic debate, poverty is reduced

---

Kinshasa

The city is also a place of great brutality, particularly for countries trau-matized by disease and war.

Witches haunt Kinshasa, the Democratic Republic of Congo's violent capital. All are children. Olivier, a nine-year-old witch, sighs, making a half-chewed, blue plastic crucifix bobble against his tummy. He knows his mother has died, but not why he has been blamed. 'I'm not a sor-cerer,' Olivier whispers, his thin skin gleaming with the telltale sheen of AIDS. 'I didn't cast any spells.' Three years ago his mother succumbed to the virus marauding through Kinshasa's slum, leaving him an orphan. An uncle took him in, but with five children of his own to feed, Olivier's was one mouth too many. Within a week he resorted to another phenomenon raging through Kinshasa's slums, accusing the child of witchcraft and casting him onto the streets. Ever since, Olivier has been scavenging for survival, begging for scraps in Kinshasa's markets, or for a few francs in its fume-filled traffic. Olivier's plight is all too common in war-ravaged Congo. According to Save the Children, of Kinshasa's estimated 30,000 street-children virtually all have been abandoned by their families, having been accused of witchcraft. ■

James Astill, *The Observer*, 11 May 2003. http://observer.guardian.co.uk

---

to simple, mechanistic formulae: you add up the cost of a 'basket' of basic necessities, take account of the income people have, and the shortfall expresses the extent and intensity of their poverty.

Unfortunately, it is not so easy.

Bureaucratic definitions

Economists, politicians, humanitarians often state that more than one billion people in the world live on less than a dollar a day, while three billion have less than $2 a day. This is quoted as proof of unspeakable deprivation. Audiences exposed to it register their shock and amazement.

But it doesn't tell the whole story. It is deceptive because it disregards the wealth of those who provide for themselves outside of the global market. A life with an income of virtually zero does not have to be degrading if people can provide all their own needs for themselves. If they grow their own food, construct their own shelters, make their own clothes, what they need to purchase in the market may be negligible.

On the other hand, an income of $200 a day may represent poverty when all needs must be answered through the market and this is insufficient for that purpose.

These accounts of poverty take too much for granted. They take a meaning of what it is to be poor in industrial society and apply it to the whole planet.

Nearly all discussions by international institutions, aid agencies and donors rely upon the false premise that poor people are defined by their relationship to the global market. The purpose of development appears to be the gradual inclusion of all peoples of the world into a single economic system. Globalization suggests exactly that. Yet there are hundreds of millions who have not fully joined the global market, or have done so only partially, or not at all. These are perceived as 'backward' or 'primitive'. It is the purpose of development to ensure they are coerced into the global market – or 'enjoy all the benefits of industrial society', whether they want them or not.

There are two flaws in such assumptions. One is that anyone excluded from the global economy must be impoverished indeed, and the second is that only economic growth can 'answer' poverty.

Poverty has a history: the story of development is also a narrative of impoverishment. In order to 'develop', people must first become poor in a particular way.

The wealth of indigenous peoples

The strongest resistance against the global economy comes from indigenous peoples, whose lives have depended directly – often for millennia – upon the resource-base of their local environment. To understand the meaning of 'sustainable' – a much-abused word – in the present world we should look not to the think-tanks of Western economists but at people who have survived in cultures which are a direct expression of the ecological niche that shelters them.

People of the Hill Tracts

Dr Khisa, 70, is a physician and historian of the Chakma tribal people in the Chittagong Hill Tracts of Bangladesh. He recalls the culture before the arrival of Bengali 'settlers'.

'There was no money in Chakma society. Tribute was paid to the Mogul kings in cotton; the Hill Tracts became known as the kingdom of cotton for that reason. In the hills *jhum* cultivation (slash-and-burn) involved paddy, *til* (sesame seed), intercropped with vegetables. Food was grown for consumption, cotton for clothing and sesame for trade. All we required from outside was salt, dry fish and earthenware for cooking and storing water. They were expert weavers, as still may be seen... They had rich supplements of food from the jungles – bamboo shoots, many varieties of yam, scores of species of fish, crabs, snails, lizards. They used bamboo fish-traps: powdered tree-bark in the water made the fish drowsy, so they swam into the traps. They knew herbal remedies, some of which have been synthesized by transnational companies. I was born in 1933: as a child I never saw a shop selling rice.' ■

Indigenous cultures everywhere tell a similar story. Their societies were not scarred by poverty. They might have been impoverished by natural catastrophe – flood, drought, cyclone – but they never degraded their own home-place. Foreign invasions into the territories of others, which were seen as 'empty' – particularly the Americas and Australasia – are a long-term consequence of colonialism. Colonialism was not an event, it was a process and it continues today.

The sustaining resource-base of forests, croplands, coastal and riverine environments has been largely destroyed, which has made people poor in a different way from a poverty that arose intermittently from the vagaries of nature. This has a vital bearing on discussions of poverty, which now take place under the auspices of global institutions. These assume that only residual populations rely for sustenance on the environment where they have thrived for centuries.

This is for many poor people a tragic mistake. All human beings depend to a great extent upon the freely given, the non-monetary exchanges of mutual support, the great reservoir of generosity and affection, the vast capacity for invention and creativity beyond material reward, the voluntarily offered gifts of humanity. This makes our lives rich beyond anything that can be bought in the market. In some societies the areas of providing for ourselves and others are extensive; in others (especially those called 'developed') they are reduced. When people grow their own food and build their own shelters they are less dependent on the market, which plays a functional – although important – role in local communities. In rich societies the market dominates: all needs are 'bought in', are not provided by the family unit or local producers.

'Development' is a journey from the former to the latter. This is the triumph of the West, which has covered the globe, initially by conquest, annexation of the lands of others, colonialism and imperialism. At the time of formal decolonization, the roots of market society and culture were already established worldwide. Socialism, to some degree, limited the growth of the global market, replacing the market by the State. Bureaucratic inefficiency and the political coercion that went with socialist systems led to the collapse of statist societies, especially the Soviet Union. This was interpreted by the West as proof that the market was the only way. Recent years have seen a more intensive promotion of the market economy. This in turn gives rise to a market society, and indeed, to a market culture. The effect on global poverty has been far-reaching.

One consequence is that all measures of poverty are now made in purely monetary terms. 'Developed' countries are the rich ones and 'developing' countries aspire to be like them. This is simplistic and deceptive. All countries are developing countries. A question rarely asked is into what are the 'developed' countries evolving?

Economic activity draws people into an endless chase beyond sufficiency. It compels people into the pursuit of MORE (economic growth) instead of the search for ENOUGH (a secure contentment), which poor people want. The indices of development (embodied in

The indigenous peoples of India

Writer Winin Pereira writes: 'Many *Warlis* (the tribal people of Northern Maharashtra in India) do not know how to read or write but have a vast store of knowledge, orally transmitted from parents to children for countless generations. Yet the dominant society equates their illiteracy with ignorance. They do not need to write, since without instant access to their knowledge they would not survive in their demanding environment. Their memories have expanded to store it reliably. Each individual is an expert in all aspects of knowledge, with very limited specialization. This, together with little division of labor, contributes much to equity.

'Raji Vavre, a 12-year-old girl, knows the names of over a hundred herbs, shrubs and trees and their varied uses. These supplement her basic diet of cereals and pulses with essential proteins, vitamins and minerals. She knows which plants are a source of fiber, which are good for fuel and lighting, which have medicinal uses. She knows how to get crabs out of their holes and how to trap fish. She can catch wild hare, quail and partridges and locate birds' nests.' ■

Winin Pereira *Asking the Earth*, Earthscan 1992. www.earthscan.co.uk

the UN Human Development Index) usually include not only monetary income but also literacy and life expectancy. These, like money-income, do not measure the full range of human riches.

This is not an argument in favor of illiteracy. It pleads for a more generous version of what it means to be rich or poor. The elasticity of memory, alertness of mind and sureness of foot of the Warlis are indices of intelligence. The crude monitors of poverty that measure only money cannot accommodate intangible, wise and beautiful accounts of human possibilities; globalization involves their extinction.

How colonialism became development

Resources in the South have been enclosed and privatized, as occurred with the commons (land held collectively) in Britain and other Western countries between the late Middle Ages and the Industrial Revolution.

Colonialism was not only for export during the

Defining poverty

British imperial period: there was no violence practised against the peoples of empire that had not already been tried and tested at home. The destruction of the culture of the Highland people of Scotland after the massacre at Culloden, the eviction of the crofters (subsistence farmers) for more profitable sheep, the enclosure of common land, which prevented rural people from grazing their animals and gathering fuel, wild fruits and nuts, destructive faith in market forces which reduced by half the population of Ireland in the 1840s – all this prefigured later colonial practice.

The assault on indigenous cultures was an extension of what Europeans had already accomplished in their own lands. Throughout industrialization in Britain popular protest grew in response to an impoverishment caused by the creation of wealth. The handloom

---

The extinction of indigenous cultures

Writing of the effects of the convict settlements in New South Wales in the 1820s upon the Aboriginals, historian Robert Hughes says: 'The decay of fringe-dwelling blacks on the edge of white urban culture – the remnants of the Iroa, Gammeraigal and Daruk – was inexorable and all-pervasive; to sympathetic onlookers it seemed a plague, and to racist ones a bestial joke. Stupefied with the cheapest grade of rum, racked with every new disease from tuberculosis to syphilis, begging and babbling in the flash-talk and gutter argot of the convicts, they were caricatures of misery.'

A century and a half later, the Figueiredo report into the treatment of the Brazilian Indians didn't even have the mitigating feature of ignorance of the involuntary settlers in Australia. 'The 5,000 page document revealed a catalogue of atrocities. It documented mass murder, torture and bacteriological warfare, reported slavery, sexual abuse, theft and neglect – mostly during the previous seven years. It was reported that groups of Pataxo Indians had been deliberately infected with smallpox; the Tapayuna were poisoned with arsenic and ant killer; the Maxacali were given alcohol by landowners whose gunmen then shot them down while they were drunk.

No-one ever went to prison for these atrocities. ■

Robert Hughes, *The Fatal Shore*, Collins Harvill, 1987.
Survival International, *Disinherited*, 2000.

---

weavers, whose work had been domestic, in which the whole family participated, were starved (sometimes literally) into the factory system. Mechanization led to the destruction of machinery by 'Luddites' (a word that has persisted in English to stigmatize anyone standing against 'progress'). There were riots and demonstrations, and sometimes the military opened fire on workers (shootings in Manchester in 1817 came to be known as Peterloo). As the historian EP Thompson wrote in *The Making of the English Working Class*, even if it can be shown that during the early 19th century the money income of people rose, the squalor of towns, the compulsory migrations of people and the loss of rural livelihood were felt as deprivation, not improvement. This is now occurring worldwide.

It has an important bearing on the brutal dispossessions of ways of life in the places where the British, French, Spanish and Dutch expressed their imperial will. They transformed non-cash economies and made them grow crops for the market. Indian farmers forced to grow indigo or cultivate opium were victims of great violence. It became impossible for them to feed their own families. These interventions disrupted ancient cultures and civilizations. People were compelled to grow crops for sale instead of subsistence: this is now 'normal' worldwide. Farmers produce coffee, tea, cocoa, bananas, pineapples, tobacco, rubber and other 'primary products'; when the prices of these decline on world markets they cannot buy back the nourishment they once easily provided for themselves. They often buy cheap processed food from the West in exchange for the asparagus, beans, green peas, broccoli, mangoes or pineapples to be found in any Western supermarket.

What colonialism did not succeed in suppressing, 'development' and globalization have continued to suppress. If the West now routinely invokes sustainability, this is in order to destroy it more effectively.

It can be understood from the above that contemporary poverty did not occur in a vacuum. It has a long, tormented history and is a consequence of half a millennium of Western dominance; a dominance which the West established at home as well as in territories of their imperial overlordship.

Bringing people to market

Global poverty has been, and is still being, recreated in the image of poverty in the West: a money calculation of what is required for survival. The trouble is, no-one can agree on what 'survival' means. For instance, a TV set is now a necessity in Europe and North America. Not because human beings need continuous entertainment, but because TV, by advertising and the display of conspicuous consumption, becomes the means of showing people things they don't have.

Appropriate development

Martin Khor, of the Consumers' Association of Penang in Malaysia, writes: 'Within each Third World nation there are still large areas where communities earn their livelihoods in ways consistent with the preservation of their culture and of their natural environment. Such communities have nearly disappeared in the developed world. We need to recognize and rediscover the technological and cultural wisdom of our indigenous systems of agriculture, industry, shelter, water and sanitation and medicine. I do not mean here the unquestioning acceptance of everything traditional in a romantic belief in a past Golden Age. For instance, exploitative feudal or slave social systems also made life more difficult in the past. But many indigenous technologies, skills and processes that are still part and parcel of Third World life and are appropriate for sustainable development had harmony with nature and the community. These indigenous scientific systems have to be accorded their proper recognition. They must be saved from being swallowed up by modernization.' ■

International Journal of Rural Studies, Vol 6 No 2, October 1999.
www.ivcs.org.uk/IJRS

These must be desired in order to participate in everyday life, which now means the semi-religious cult of consumerism.

This sets everyone on earth on the same developmental path. The norms of the market economy are globalized. It ensures all other ways of answering need will continue to be eroded and the free gifts of nature and humanity alike will be transformed into commodities. Tribal peoples, dwellers in forests and jungles, aboriginal peoples who survived the first great onslaught of imperialism are now being compelled into the global economy. It ensures that as the peoples of the world abandon their ancient ways of living they enter without choice into the global market.

Once measures of wealth and poverty depend solely on money, poverty becomes incurable. The rich are hooked forever upon the boundless growth of the agent of their enrichment and no longer know the meaning of 'enough'. The ancient dream of 'sufficiency' is lost.

Enclosed within the market economy, people learn how to be poor according to its rules and laws. Concerned reformers who speak of the scandal of people living on less than a dollar a day are actually

World Health Organization Fact Sheet No 134, revised May 2003 www.who.int

Traditional medicines

Despite the overwhelming global influence of the Western medical model, the use of traditional medicines (TM) continues.

Percentage of

Births which the World Health Organization estimates were (positively) assisted by traditional birth attendants in several African countries	50+
TM in total medicinal consumption in China	30+
Population in rich countries that has used TM at least once	50+
People living with HIV/AIDS in San Francisco, London and South Africa who have used TM	70
Population of Germany who have used TM at some point in their life	90

saying something else. They are saying that such sad souls are excluded from the market economy and must be brought within its cold embrace as soon as possible. Another way of looking at people who have not yet entered the market economy is to say that they remain free. They are independent.

I spoke to a farmer in the mid 1990s on the Malaysian island of Langkawi. At that time the island was beginning the 'development' that turned it into a sought-after tourist destination. This farmer's land was being taken compulsorily by government for part of a golf course for visitors. He said bitterly: 'The only people in the world who are truly free are those who can grow their own food. My land has yielded a harvest ever since anyone can remember. Next year it will give its last harvest – a handful of dollars. After that it will be barren and I and my family will be poor.'

Those still living partly or wholly outside of the global market give the lie to the claim that there is no alternative to a single world economy. Such people are dangerous economic dissidents. Their punishment is to be locked into the global system at the lowest level of survival, where they will learn the hard way new meanings of poverty.

Tyranny

This is tyranny – which is why it is called 'freedom' by the powerful, who have decided the whole world will live according to their rules. To extinguish alternatives is as intolerant as it is violent. Globalization is ideology made material: ideology not as theory but in relentless, inflexible practice. To say: 'There is no market for it' – whether 'it' means some commodity or service, or whether it means compassion, wisdom, self-sacrifice or some form of artistic expression – is to condemn areas of vital human experience to silence and non-existence.

The struggle to establish the dominance of a world

market is an attack not only upon the poor but upon all people whose life-ways and strategies for answering need, whose independence, in short, is a reproach to the impoverishing modes of enrichment brought by the global market.

Ever since the age of imperialism, low-intensity warfare has been waged against self-reliance. In recent years its battle-cry has been 'development'. Its weaponry has been money. Its foot soldiers have been the high-consuming middle class, which has emerged in every country in the world. Its members are both ambassadors and police of the version of the good life as defined by the industrialized world.

Modernizing

The market 'modernizes' poverty, in the words of Ivan Illich. It replaces resource poverty with money poverty. In consequence, poverty can no longer be measured. You know precisely how much land is needed to grow sufficient food; but no-one has ever satisfactorily judged how much money is needed to heal the subjective feeling of being poor. As long as human beings retain control over the resources – land, materials, seeds – they require for their sustenance, they are not poor. They may be victims of external circumstances, warfare, flood, drought, but that is different from bondage to a global market controlled from elsewhere.

When the institutions and representatives of privileged people speak of 'poverty alleviation' they never mean the return of control over resources to the people. They invariably refer to money, to 'income-generating capacities', to loans or microcredit (which often means grooming them for the market by means of indebtedness). This incorporates people into a global system from which there is no exit.

The market teaches us what we do not have. Through self-reliance we discover what we need.

Defining poverty

And that is surprisingly little. Through the market economy and its engines of publicity and advertising we learn what we might get. The market serves the growing self-consciousness of an industrialized humanity which has learned to think of satisfactions in mechanistic terms. 'Getting' and 'having' submerge being, and undermine a judicious, restrained use of the fruits of earth. The global market makes us understand that all that is homemade and self-created, the familiar artifacts and goods of traditional culture, the homely values of the locally produced, are junk; that what is machine-produced, perfect and flawless, has superior value. Cheap mass-produced imports displace goods made from local materials: bamboo gives way to plastic, *chetai* (adobe/mud) to cement, thatch to tiles.

Each new thing that appears in the market makes irrelevant all previous ways of answering need; it allows skills, human effort and achievement to fall into decay. Its very 'efficiency' in allocating goods and services to those who can afford them is the enemy of creative purpose.

Is this why the great shopping malls that bestride every community in the Western world (and many in the South as well) exercise such a fascination over peoples everywhere? In all countries, at whatever stage of 'development', people shake their heads as new commodities reach the market – and they remember when these purchased necessities were answered from within their own competence.

Peasants are scandalized by the price in the market of staple foods which they grew on their own *shamba*; the urban poor are shocked by wasted food that perishes in the shops for want of buyers; people in the rich world see the wastefulness of buying-in ready-made meals, when preparing food is such a simple chore. In the West an older generation recalls when 'we made our own fun' and knew how to entertain and amuse one another. Their grandchildren look upon them with an estranged pity, wondering how anyone could live without computer games, perpetual music and the flickering images which give meaning to their own lives.

It is not that people become greedy or selfish but that we inhabit a system which has disgraced frugality and restraint. Our way of life institutionalizes perpetual growth and expansion: the limitlessness of human desire is harnessed to an infinity of economic growth. And then we marvel at the persistence of poverty, not only in those parts of the world still called 'third', but in the richest societies that have ever existed on earth!

Whatever the cultural tradition in which people have defined poverty, everyone in the world is emerging into a global market which describes poverty solely in terms of purchasing power. This process is itself a form of impoverishment, for it means all other, imaginative responses of human beings to their own and others' needs are marginalized and fall into disuse. The market offers people unlimited 'freedom to choose' (as long as they have the money) within its own version of plenty; but in doing so it snuffs out profounder freedoms. At its crudest, the choice between 130 forms of shampoo is offered in exchange for our lost liberties.

The judges

Rather than poor people defining their needs, assessments of poverty have remained in the hands of professionals and experts – those who want to relieve it, measure it, punish people for it, even make it worse.

A simple account of basic needs can readily be drawn up. This is a useful guide to survival, but few people live in such a state of abstract social and cultural nakedness. Indeed, it is the very simplicity of our needs that make them sound so thin when taken out of context. If we speak of food, water, shelter, clothing, healthcare, education, social and affective relationships, play and leisure, as well as a sense of purpose and meaning, these are easily answerable, yet curiously void of content.

It is only for the poor that programs are drawn up claiming to answer their basic needs. No-one dreams of offering the rich such a reductive version of what they might need. This is a source of many of the problems associated with discussions of basic needs.

Cultures grow organically. Customs and practices, traditions and taboos, rituals and festivals evolve. They do so in a way that conceals and decorates the bare facts of our existence – that we live and die, love, give birth and age. No-one lives in naked contemplation of the predictable simplicity of our human destiny.

To offer poor people answers to their needs is an act of enormous condescension. It can be justified only at times of emergency – in the wake of disaster, earthquakes, floods, in war or civil conflict, when people are driven from their homes and survive outside cultural norms and expectations. Tent cities of refugees fleeing war in DR Congo or Afghanistan, people in temporary centers following floods in Mozambique or Bangladesh, the frightened inhabitants of Chechnya or Gaza City, refugees from famine – only in such circumstances do 'basic needs' make sense.

However, in the early years of the 21st century we are living at a moment of extreme polarization between rich and poor. The consequences of this are becoming daily more plain: global security is imperiled, wars are waged over basic commodities such as water, not to mention oil or land. We are living through a time, not of some local emergency, but of possible worldwide catastrophe. This gives new urgency to the question: what constitutes enough for our sustenance? What needs to be done for everyone on earth, not to grow rich, but to acquire a dignified sufficiency? There is a crisis in the only model of progress now on offer.

This task is made more difficult precisely because the fundamental purpose of the economy, society and culture of the West is accumulation and increase, growth and expansion for their own sake. Such a society is not ideally placed to measure whether or not its own basic needs have been answered, let alone those of anybody else.

If the needs of all people on earth are to be provided for, this must also include those in high-consuming societies as well as those on the edge of survival. Indeed, we should begin with the privileged themselves, since it is by their norms and values that the people of the world live or die, achieve fulfillment or perish. Poverty is caused not by 'scarce resources' or a world of insufficiency, but by wealth; or rather, by the particular form wealth has taken in an unequal, unjust global society.

Human need is at war with economic necessity. This is true for both rich and poor.

The global economic system has become autonomous, human well-being an incidental by-product of its workings. The most flamboyant wealth coexists with the wretchedness of two-thirds of humanity. Wealth is not designed to 'answer' poverty, but to reproduce itself endlessly – a monstrous mimicry of life itself.

Other forms of poverty

This far from exhausts the meanings of poverty. It takes no account of the freely chosen poverty of a religious institution, renunciations of the spirit. It ignores voluntary simplicity, the efforts by people in the rich world to live more sparingly, with what Ilich calls 'a joyful austerity'. Collective and communitarian groups who pool resources, both human and material, to live modestly, offer another view of poverty from

Shapla Sundheri

She is a small, laughing woman in her early 70s. She lives in a tiny cell-like room in an ashram in Vrindavan, a town 120 kilometers from Delhi. The only furniture is a narrow bed, a small mat and a cupboard. She is from a former royal family in what is now Bangladesh. She came to the ashram after her husband's death. In her room Shapla has built a shrine to Krishna: a box covered with shiny gold and silver paper. Inside, a little lamp, and above, a picture of Krishna and a frieze of dancing *gopis* (milkmaids). In front of the shrine she has placed a bowl of milk, some slices of coconut, a banana and some water in a metal tumbler. Today is a day of fast, which she will break with the food purified by the presence of her lord. A woman with nothing can also be happy. ∎

HelpAge India, 2002

the raw relentless want of dispossessed peasant and unemployed slum-dweller.

It also fails to acknowledge the significance of 'deprivation', which is sometimes used to express poverty in the rich world. This is a very accurate expression, for it says that some people are 'deprived', which means something is taken away or withheld from them. In other words, like 'dispossession', it implies human agency – somebody has deprived somebody else of what is needful for a decent life.

When speaking of 'deprivation' the first question to ask is: who has done the depriving and who is advantaged by it? It is not only a question of what 'we must do'; there is also a 'they', who are beneficiaries of other people's impoverishment.

1 Frances Moore Lappé, *World Hunger: Twelve Myths*, Grove Atlantic/Food First, 1998. **2** UN International Fund for Agricultural Development, 2000.

4 The mechanisms of impoverishment

From colonialism to 'development' and the globalization of market culture; the institutions of poverty, debt and trade; privatizing necessities; the politics of Poverty Reduction Strategies; the tenderness of the rich.

'Poverty wants some, luxury many, and avarice all things.'
Seneca

GLOBAL POVERTY IS not a matter of lack of resources but a consequence of economic control by the rich countries. How this came about remains a story largely untold by the historians of privilege.

Globalization (the integration, to varying degrees, of all countries into a single world economic system) shows remarkable continuity with colonialism. For this, too, was an attempt by the great powers from the 16th to the 19th centuries to take over the wealth and 'raw materials' of the world, and to open up markets for their own products. It was a taste of things to come: European military power conquered peoples, many of whom had never known a money economy, and took the treasures of forests and croplands, minerals, artifacts and the finest ornaments of ancient civilizations.

The rise of Communism and the liberation movements in the colonized territories checked the imperial project after 1945. Most countries governed by the European empires chose socialism at the time of their independence. The world divided into two camps, and the struggle was on for the destiny of humankind, between the socialist and the capitalist model.

Since imperialism was identified with capitalism, the West had to produce a convincing alternative to a socialism which promised social justice and equality. This is how 'development' was born. It was an ideological construct, rooted in the historical moment in which it was conceived.

In January 1949 US President Harry S Truman declared: 'We must embark on a new program for making the benefits of our scientific advances with industrial progress available for the improvement and growth of the underdeveloped areas.' In a single sentence Truman consigned more than half of humanity to backwardness. The cultural richness and diversity of the world, its ancient patterns of life became, not a reason for celebration, but a problem – the object of a Western project of redemption.

'Development', then, was a strategy, formulated at the beginning of the Cold War. The competitive battle with Communism (which broke out in open warfare in Korea and Vietnam) was to last until the Soviet Union disintegrated in 1990. Over time, 'development' became a showy display of affluence, in contrast to the austerity associated with socialist economies.

Bangladeshi economist Anisur Rahman recognized this early on. 'It was the threat of Bolshevik revolution inspiring social revolutions in the Third World that was countered by a promise of "development" to help the underdeveloped societies to catch up with the "developed". Development was defined exclusively as economic development, reducing the degree of progress and maturity in a society to be measured by the level of its production.'[1]

'Development' evokes organic growth, flowering and maturation, not only of the human being but of nature itself – a process inherent in the very birth of 'new' countries in Asia and Africa. It also smuggled in the idea that 'underdeveloped' countries were infants, their destiny was to grow up like those which had once cast themselves as 'mother-countries'. Thus racism continued to dominate Western attitudes towards the countries they had dispossessed in the colonial period. The concept of 'emerging' countries strengthened a sense of dateless non-being out of which they had come – darkness, ignorance, the womb. The association of development with 'growth' made it easy to identify it with constant economic expansion.

The creation of wealth was central to the Western model. It seemed obvious that a system which could produce so much would easily abolish poverty. The accumulation of goods masked other realities – for instance, that the richest societies in the world were increasingly blemished by crime, violence, addictions, social breakdown and psychic disorder. In other words, the true cost of its version of riches did not appear in the apparent price.

Many Third World leaders were suspicious of the change of heart of former imperialists. They sought to vary, but not to question, the basic developmental paradigm. They came up with 'human development', 'indigenous development', 'participatory development', building on the capacities of their peoples. A more recent form is 'sustainable development', which the West has re-colonized: it now means whatever the rich can get away with. Since then, 'post-development' has emerged, with its suggestion that we are already living in a kind of blessed afterlife.

While development was pitted against its socialist rival, its promises remained largely in the realm of fantasy. Poor people regarded it with skepticism, concerned as they were with filling their bellies, finding shelter from the monsoon rains, clean water, healthcare and the safe passage through childhood of a new generation.

The existence of the alternative – Communism – held the world in frozen immobility for half a century. The dissolution of the USSR, however, didn't only vanquish the rival to 'development'. It also called the bluff of the developmental mirage that the West had promoted. The time had come for the world to call in the promises made in the heat of rivalry. Could they be realized? Could the West deliver?

The benefits of the Western way of wealth are not in doubt, although they remain out of reach for the majority of humanity. Everywhere in the world people have voted with their feet, seeking out the golden realms of peace and plenty. Graduates from all over the South queue up to work as houseboys or maidservants in Jeddah or Abu Dhabi, as factory labor in economic priority zones all over Asia, as fast-food servers in the have-a-nice-day culture of Europe and North America. Some have traveled in leaky boats to pick potatoes or beet in the icy winter dawns of Northern Europe or, packed into refrigerated containers and suffocating trucks, sometimes perished in pursuit of oppressive labor at destinations they never reached.

It has seemed to more and more people that the good things promised will not come to them: these would have to be sought out in the places where they have accumulated in bewildering profusion.

The epic migrations of our time are a response to promises of modernization and progress. Are the caravans of hope now crossing the world following pathways to prosperity, or merely tracing to its source the agent of their impoverishment? There is a severe prohibition on economic migrants, painted as the chancers and opportunists of the world, who seek to pass through barriers made porous by globalization. Suffering peoples, once lured by promises of improvement so that they should not be tempted by the doubtful attractions of socialism, now face barbed wire, No Entry signs and armed guards at the corners of closed-off avenues of global mobility.

The flaws in the capitalist model, concealed by the glaring defects of its ideological rival, are now clearer. The West will share with the world, not its wealth but the mysteries of its capacity for wealth-creation. The messages, however, omit certain details, the most important being that the West grew rich by the exploitation of the very territories and peoples it now exhorts to follow in its footsteps. Indeed, the best-kept secret of 'development' is that it is a colonial concept, a project of extraction. Since most countries have no colonial possessions from which wealth may be squeezed, they must place intolerable pressure on their own people and environment. The rights of minorities are violated, the resource-base of forest people and subsistence farmers plundered to earn foreign exchange, the labor of the poor sold to the lowest bidder, 'surplus population' moved as settlers into ancestral homelands of tribal and indigenous peoples.

A system of limitless economic expansion in a limited world – this is the ideology of development. It is no more capable of being realized now than it was when inhibited by the controls of socialism.

Perhaps market culture will reach all the inhabitants of a world ransacked of its treasures. If it does so, it will be changed in transmission. Poor people can expect consumerism instead of relief from poverty, economic growth instead of security, Coca-Cola rather than safe water, junk food instead of adequate nutrition, instruction from commerce in lieu of education, products of entertainment conglomerates as a substitute for ancient cultures.

How long they will tolerate this version of 'development' devised in another era, as a diversion from the appeal of socialism, is a question to which answers are already being provided by some of the humiliated and excluded.

Institutionalizing development
Unfair development has been institutionalized. It lies in the mechanisms that 'manage' globalization, including the International Monetary Fund (IMF)

and World Bank (two of the 'Bretton Woods' institutions), the Asian Development Bank, the World Trade Organization, transnational companies and governments of the rich countries. These preach a fictitious doctrine of 'free' markets.

'Freedom' in the economic sphere is code for whatever advantages the world's wealthy people. Free trade is no such thing. Poor farmers in the South cannot compete with the European Union and America, whose governments pay vast subsidies to their own food producers. 'Free markets', similarly, are a myth. Money moves freely around the world at a touch of a button, and some commodities may move too (subject to quotas and tariffs), but human beings (or 'labor', as they appear in the economic calculus) are severely controlled – as panic over 'economic migrants' in Europe shows.

The IMF and World Bank were set up at the end of World War Two to help reconstruct Europe after the ravages of war. They were to provide unconditional loans to avoid economic crises and to steady exchange rates. The growth of these institutions was phenomenal: they financed infrastructural and

---

The Highly Indebted Poor Countries Initiative (HIPC)

In 1996 the HIPC was launched to reduce the debts of the poorest countries to sustainable levels. As a result of extensive campaigning by Jubilee 2000, the HIPC was extended at the G-7 (rich-countries) summit in Cologne in 1999, with a pledge of $100 billion of debt relief.

This was barely one-third of the amount Jubilee 2000 considered essential. Not all donor countries have fulfilled their promise and 'sustainable' levels of debt have not been delivered. Malawi, which owes $2.9 billion, is eligible for $950 million, but even the remaining debt is beyond its capacity to repay. Although experiencing a crisis of both hunger and HIV/AIDS, Malawi is still expected to pay $66 million a year, mainly to the rich countries, the IMF and World Bank. ■

Jubilee Research, www.jubilee2000uk.org.

developmental projects in the South in the 1960s, became agents for recycling the capital generated by oil price increases of the 1970s. They provided the loans to the countries of the South which created the debt crisis. The IMF moved in with structural-adjustment programs which pressured countries to export more in order to 'service' that debt, even if this meant increasing poverty.

Debt is a major tool for control. The indebtedness of people of the West keeps them in line: students leaving university owe thousands of dollars for an education already consumed; people will 'own' their houses courtesy of a 'redemption day' 25 years hence. Everything, from the goods people take on credit to the pensions they hope to enjoy, ties individuals to a global financial system. How much more powerful is debt in attaching whole countries to a global order from which there is no escape!

Under the neoliberal ideology of the 1980s (the 'Washington Consensus'), the IMF became the enforcer of the integration of all countries into the global economy. The answer to debt was further loans and new 'conditionalities' – liberalizing the economy, opening up domestic markets to competition, deregulation, devaluation of the currency (to increase 'competitiveness') and cuts in government spending (except on arms, purchased mostly from the 'advanced' industrial countries). These cuts were overwhelmingly in healthcare, education, nutrition and welfare services, which impoverished people already poor. Indebted countries were also compelled to export more to 'earn' the money to 'honor' the debt. Since many compete in exporting primary commodities like coffee, sugar, cocoa, or manufactured goods like garments, shoes and toys, prices are continuously falling. They must then export more and more to earn the same amount.

Jubilee 2000 campaigned worldwide for the G-7 and financial institutions to forgive the debt of the poorest countries: 24 million people signed the largest petition ever seen. By the end of the campaign in December 2000 it was clear that debt cancellation didn't match the rhetoric of the powerful. The Jubilee Debt Campaign is the successor to Jubilee 2000 and carries forward the pressure on decision-makers for debt cancellation and poverty reduction. The movement has a base in many countries across the world.

Identical programs were forced upon all countries by the IMF, increasing debt and dependency. In parallel, negotiations of the General Agreement on Tariffs and Trade became institutionalized in the World Trade Organization (WTO) in 1995. This was supposed to set up a rules-based system for implementing global compliance with a highly skewed version of 'free trade'. Poor countries would have to open themselves up to the rich countries for agricultural imports and industrial manufactures, as well as to the service sector, not only in finance and banking but also electricity, water and power, telecommunications and the 'cultural products' of media conglomerates.

The effects of 'free' trade

Criticism of the mechanisms that keep poor countries poor has led to a continuous shift in the rhetoric, if not the practice, of the financial institutions. Ever since the World Bank was accused of aiding projects that damage local people – the transmigration program in Indonesia, the Pernambuco dam in Brazil – it has shown constant remorse and promised to reform. You want environmental protection? This is our priority. You want gender equality? We were just going to suggest it. You want participatory development? It was on the tip of our tongue. You want good governance? It is our most urgent concern. Now, poverty abatement is the slogan of the hour.

Similarly, the IMF claims it has listened and learned from popular protest around the world. Yet it is still imposing the same conditions and impossible burdens that led to the débâcle in Argentina, where half the population was plunged into poverty thanks to the (contradictory) prescriptions of the IMF.

Structural adjustment programs, lowered living standards, increased poverty, falling wages and rising prices have led to riots in many countries. Capital then takes flight and deserts the places where ungrateful people find it difficult to understand that the economic health of the country depends upon their own deteriorating well-being. This happened in the Asian crisis of 1998, in Russia and in Mexico. At this point the financial institutions blame corrupt governments, cronyism and collusion: the élites upon whom they forced their advice become guilty of betraying their own people.

The World Development Movement publishes an annual report on popular protests around the world. In 2001 it documented protests in 23 poor countries against their governments' economic policies, recording 77 incidents of civil unrest involving millions of people. Eighteen of these led to the deployment of riot police or the army, with 76 documented fatalities; arrests and injuries ran into thousands. Over a third of these countries experienced protests specifically directed at the IMF and World Bank.

Competition

Competition between countries for investment from multinational companies leads them to a Dutch auction of the labor of their people. One result is that garments bought in the shopping malls of the West are stitched in makeshift factories that have sprung up in free-trade zones, where labor laws are suspended and human rights abrogated. They draw children and women into secretive sweatshops guarded by soldiers and police against intrusive inspection.

In 1993, under the Harkin Bill, the US threatened to

cease importing garments from Bangladesh made with child labor. Whether this was altruism on the part of the US or a form of protectionism is another question. It certainly had its effect. Within months the factories were emptied of children, at least temporarily. When I visited a factory in Dhaka in the late 1990s I arrived just in time to see the children being locked into the toilet.

Commodities are still the main export of the poorest countries. 'Advanced' countries export sophisticated products and import commodities, while the poorest import value-added goods from the rich. The foreign exchange from exported timber, sugar or coffee constantly decreases in value, so poor producers are always disadvantaged.

The rice farmers of Haiti

Phillippe Michel works in a rice mill in Haiti's Artibonite Valley. The mill was built so that poor farmers could process their rice before taking it to market. But when the markets in the capital, Port-au-Prince, are awash with cheap imported rice, buyers don't bother to travel to Artibonite to purchase Haitian rice.

For decades rice has provided tens of thousands of Artibonite families with a livelihood and an income. Now the valley's farmers are selling their land and heading off: to the shanty towns of Port-au-Prince, to the Dominican Republic for work, or risking their lives trying to enter the US illegally. Phillippe has lost a friend and a cousin that way.

Why the switch in Artibonite's fortunes? Trade rules, of course.

Successive Haitian Governments have had to eliminate restrictions on imported goods. This has prompted a flood of cheap, imported rice, mostly from the US, where arable farmers are subsidized to the tune of nearly $5 billion a year.

Haitian farmers simply can't compete: their subsidies are capped by the World Trade Organization.

Fenol Leon, an Artibonite farmer, says: 'Unless we are protected from cheap rice imports I don't think there's a future for us – we'll all be wiped out.'

Beverley Duckworth, Head of Campaigns at the World Development Movement, says: 'International trade rules must allow countries to promote food security and to protect poor farmers from unfairly subsidized food imports.' ∎

World Development Movement, 2002. www.wdm.org.uk

Despite international commitment to poverty reduction, the workings of the global economy, supported by the opaque operations of official agencies, have the opposite effect. This is the ideology

Terms of trade

In 1964 French writer René Dumont *said:*

'The terms of trade have already fallen: from 1955 to 1959 export prices went down 15 per cent, entailing a loss to tropical Africa of $600 million, twice the annual amount of foreign aid. If tropical Africa continues to orient itself towards exports, the collapse of the coffee market will undoubtedly be followed quite soon by that of cocoa, sisal and bananas, and then cotton, peanuts, tea and a good many other products.'

In 2002 a report from Guatemala said:

'In just two years, Central America has lost over $1,500 million in income from coffee exports. While the region's governments, coffee farmers and harvesters have suffered drastic reductions in income and job availability, large transnational companies involved in the final sale of the bean have increased their earnings, partly due to the fall in prices.

'In less than eight years, world coffee prices have fallen 74 per cent, from $1.82 to $0.47 per pound of unroasted coffee. At a meeting of the International Coffee Organization in May 2002 it was stated that "the current crisis is the worst in memory" and that producers' meager income could cause "explosive" social and political effects.

'Some producers in Central America are reported to have turned to farming illicit crops, while in Mexico producers have abandoned their farms, creating further migratory pressures. In Guatemala, according to a study by the International Migratory Organization, 70 per cent of workers interviewed in the coffee sector expressed an intention to migrate to the US as a result of the crisis.

'Meanwhile Proctor and Gamble, Philip Morris, Sara Lee and Nestlé, who together control 60 per cent of the US coffee market and 40 per cent of the global market, have sustained no loss. In 2000, world coffee sales generated $55 billion. Of this, the producer countries obtained $8 billion, 14.4 per cent of the bean's global sales.

'85 per cent of Central America's coffee producers are classified as micro and small producers, utilizing 27 per cent of coffee-dedicated lands and generating a quarter of production. The largest plantations are owned by 1 per cent of all producers, and produce 37 per cent of the region's coffee.' ∎

René Dumont, *False Start in Africa*, André Deutsch, 1964.
Central America Report, *Guatemala*, June 2002.

of development in operation.

Occasionally it becomes apparent to the world that this is no accident. A notorious memorandum issued by Lawrence Summers, chief economist at the World Bank, revealed the mindset of those in charge of economic affairs, and the priority they give to economics over human well-being. He argued:

'Just between you and me, shouldn't the World Bank be encouraging more migration of dirty industries to the less developed countries? ... The economic logic behind dumping a load of toxic waste in the lowest wage country is impeccable, and we should face up to that... Underpopulated countries in Africa are vastly under-polluted; their air quality is probably vastly inefficiently low compared to Los Angeles or Mexico City... the concern over an agent that causes a one in a million change in the odds of prostate cancer is obviously going to be much higher in a country where people survive to get prostate cancer than in a country where under-five mortality is 200 in a thousand.'

A recent example of this thinking is the US Government's response to the AIDS epidemic in Africa. The drug companies Pfizer, Bristol-Myers Squibb, Abbot Laboratories, Merck & Co, which manufacture the anti-retroviral drugs (ARVs) that inhibit the progress of AIDS, were major donors to George W Bush's election campaign in 2000. At a meeting of the World Trade Organization (WTO) in Doha in November 2001 it was agreed that the poorest countries be permitted to buy cheaper drugs in the interests of public health.

The Bush Administration is pressuring countries which make cheaper versions of the anti-AIDS drugs to observe the rigorous patent laws designed to protect 'intellectual property rights'. Despite the administration's donation of $15 billion to alleviate AIDS, it is threatening producer countries of very much cheaper 'generic' drugs with economic sanctions if they export them to Africa at prices that undercut those of the main transnational companies. Jean-Pierre Garnier, CEO of GlaxoSmithKline, says: 'This is an economic war. There are a couple of pirate companies who want to undermine the patent system... They would prosper by pirating our discoveries.'[2]

Structural adjustments that reduce health budgets in Africa at the same time as the AIDS pandemic grows adjust more and more people out of life itself.

The promise to the countries of the South was that if they followed the pathway 'we' showed, they would 'become like us'. Yet the path indicated to them is very different from that pursued by the West.

For one thing, popular struggle against the economic and social violence of early industrialism in the West led to organized resistance – the labor and trade-union movements, socialist political parties. This compelled governments to provide protection for people against the ravages of free markets and was institutionalized in the welfare state. Although the IMF and World Bank speak of 'safety nets' for the poor, cuts in government spending fall precisely on the very safety nets they are also supposed to provide.

There is one rule for the G-7 (richest countries) and another for the South. The G-7 now preaches open economies and liberalization, as well as 'good governance' and 'transparency'. Yet none of these

Life chances: Malawi and Britain compared

	Malawi	Britain
Population	10.7 million	59.7 million
Per capita income	$170	$14,143
HIV incidence	15%	0.1%
Numbers with HIV	1 million	34,000
AIDS deaths in 2001	80,000	460
Life expectancy	39 years	77.99 years
Health spending 2002	$52 million	$73 billion

things was conspicuous when the West grew rich. In Britain industrialization took place without democracy. It was constructed on the wealth extracted from empire and never had the slightest pretensions to free trade. After 1945 Japan became industrially powerful thanks to government protection for its growing industrial base.

Most Western countries provide basic welfare for their most vulnerable, medical care for the aged, support for the long-term sick and disabled, and for those thrown out of work by cyclical or structural economic change.

Yet the South is expected to develop without such protection. It is instructed to open itself up to organizations even more powerful than governments – multinational companies which in some cases have a turnover greater than the country in which they are investing. In 2000 the Institute of Policy Studies revealed that of the world's largest 100 economic entities, 51 are now corporations and 49

The mistake

In 2002 Joseph Stiglitz, former chief economist at the World Bank, published a penitential critique of the role of the World Bank, but especially of the IMF and the WTO. About IMF-inspired programs he writes: 'The application of mistaken (sic) economic theories would not be such a problem if the end of first colonialism and then communism had not given the IMF and the World Bank the opportunity to greatly expand their respective original mandates, to vastly extend their reach. Today these institutions have become dominant players in the world economy. Not only countries seeking their help but also those seeking their "seal of approval" so that they can better access international financial markets must follow their economic prescriptions, which reflect their free-market ideologies and theories. The result for many people has been poverty and for many countries social and political chaos. The IMF has made mistakes in all areas it has been involved in: development, crisis management, and in countries in transition from communism to capitalism.' ∎

Joseph Stiglitz, *Globalization and its Discontents*, Allen Lane, 2002.

countries. The 22 largest entities are countries, with Turkey just ahead of General Motors. After Denmark follow Wal-Mart, ExxonMobil, Ford Motor and DaimlerChrysler. Indonesia and Greece are slightly ahead of Mitsui, Mitsubishi, Toyota, General Electric, Itochu and Royal Dutch/Shell, which are all bigger than Venezuela, Iran and Israel.[3]

Democracy, too, is undermined by the work of the IMF and World Bank. Over and above the welfare of people, giving priority to foreign investors and financial markets is the price paid by governments of the South for 'stability'. Indeed, this is often a precondition of their 'electability'. Countries like Cuba, which refuse to follow the Western model, have been the object of sabotage and continuous propaganda. Life is easier for élites of the countries that go along with the 'advice' offered by their Western mentors.

After all, the interests of ruling classes everywhere coincide. The rewards from the privatization of public assets fill their pockets, permit them to travel abroad for healthcare (their own systems being inadequate), to send their children to study in the US or Europe (their own education system being run down by neglect), to own property in California or London (in case they are ever driven into exile by ungrateful electorates).

The World Bank and the IMF are controlled by the governments of the world's richest countries. The G-7 together have more than 40 per cent of the directors' votes. The US holds 16.45 per cent of the votes at the World Bank and 17 per cent of those at the IMF. Since an 85-per-cent majority is required for the most important decisions, the US effectively has the power of veto.

The Bretton Woods Project (an organization set up specifically for the reform of the IMF and World Bank) revealed that an 'internal World Bank report – *The Effect of the IMF and World Bank on Poverty* by William Easterly – has concluded that the poor are better off without structural adjustment'. The report says the poor 'may be ill-placed to take advantage of the opportunities created by structural adjustment programs', which suggests it is the fault of poor people themselves – for being so uneducated and unskilled.[4]

The healers

At the Millennium Summit in New York in 2000, 149 heads of State, the European Union, the International Monetary Fund and World Bank resolved to halve the numbers of people in the world living in abject poverty by 2015. This was defined as those living on less than a dollar a day; an aspiration repeated at the Sustainable Development Summit in Johannesburg in September 2002, where concern of business and corporate care for the poor was also conspicuously proclaimed.

In December 2000 the British Government published a 'White Paper' committing itself to work with others 'to manage globalization so that poverty is systematically reduced and international development targets realized'.

This document mixes pieties and platitudes. Its purpose, like that of the Millennium Summit, is to wrench any definition of the needs of the poor from poor people themselves and to reformulate them in terms that serve the interests of the rich.

The transformation of the Bretton Woods institutions into instruments of dispossession has already been noted. In view of the inequalities to which their policies have contributed over the past 60 years, it is strange that they are now being promoted as healers of poverty. Yet it seems to surprise no-one that bankers are now overcome by affection for the poor, or that moneylenders exhibit great tenderness for their victims.

According to the White Paper, the strategy for

managing globalization is 'to promote economic growth that is equitable and environmentally sustainable'. Into these ten words are packed every contradiction of all discussions on development of the past half century.

The creation of wealth without redistribution increases inequality. As wealth grows so the 'poverty line' rises. By 2015 the goods and services that can be obtained for one dollar today may cost three or five dollars. The numbers living on less than a dollar a day may have been halved, but this will give no indication of how much better-off they are or, indeed, whether they are better off at all.

The White Paper acknowledges many of the factors which exacerbate poverty: 'War and conflict, movement of refugees, violation of human rights, international crime, terrorism, the drugs trade, health pandemics and environmental degradation.'

It could be argued that these scourges are caused or aggravated by wealth: wars funded by diamonds in Africa, for instance, are not caused by the love of African peasants for the glittering stones on their elegant fingers.

Refugees displaced by dams, roads, industrial infrastructure, airports, agribusiness, land-grabbing, evictions and debt are victims of the greed of the world's wealthy people.

International crime is big business – the fact that big business is increasingly international crime is not, apparently, a cause for concern, despite the criminality of a host of companies revealed in 2002 – Enron, Global Crossing and WorldCom among them.

Environmental degradation by logging companies, mining conglomerates, industrial fishing and chemical agriculture are not mentioned, yet these damage the global environment more violently than the poor, forced to find fuel, food and fodder at the margins of the biosphere.

The mechanisms of impoverishment

Human rights are particularly cherished by the West, which has never acknowledged economic rights. Human rights mean freedom from political oppression, tyranny and abuse, while economic oppression, tyranny and abuse are built into the very structures of globalization.

After conceding that the transnational companies now account for one-third of global output, two-thirds of trade (one-third of it between the companies themselves), the White Paper states: 'Managed wisely, the new wealth creates opportunities to lift the poor out of poverty, but it depends upon policy choices by governments, international institutions, the private sector and civil society.'

In this version of the world, wealth is clean. It uses non-polluting technologies. The poor damage the environment. Sustainable development doesn't mean taking from the earth no more than we put back, it means bringing to the poor the model of development on which 'we' grew rich. But the telecommunications industry of Bangladesh or the power companies of Indonesia are not going to take over the assets of the US or Japan. Indian armaments are not going to flood the markets of Europe, nor Filipino fast-foods chase out McDonald's or KFC/Kentucky Fried Chicken.

'Where there are no rules', says the British Government, 'the rich and powerful bully the poor and powerless.' But when the rules are those of the rich and powerful, institutional arrangements will do what is necessary to maintain the status quo. 'Poor countries need effective, open and accountable global institutions where they can pursue their interests on more equal terms.' None of this characterizes the institutions set up by the West, the IMF and World Bank. When Western governments have routinely given material help and comfort to some of the most brutal tyrannies – didn't they support Mobuto and Idi Amin, Suharto and Marcos, Zia ul-Haq and

Stroessner, not to mention Saddam Hussein? – it may strike one as a little hypocritical to call others to good governance and campaigns against corruption.

The tenderness of the rich

When care for poor people is passed over to the agencies which have impoverished them the consequences are predictable.

In keeping with the politics of appearances, the IMF has re-branded its Structural Adjustment Program as Poverty Reduction Growth Facility, and its Policy Framework Papers as Poverty Reduction Strategy Papers. This allows it to continue its labor undisturbed. Governments sign up to the same policies and duly transmit the superintendence of them to those who deal with poor people on the ground.

By means of impersonal 'free' economic forces the war on poverty becomes a war on the poor. And the preferred method is commonly used in the rich world – poor people must be made to disappear. The simplest way to do this in the South is by eviction – from the land they occupy, from the fragile settlements they have constructed, from the livelihoods of a precarious survival.

Despite the Universal Declaration of Human Rights, it is not a human right:

- To eat: as starvation deaths in Rajasthan in India in 2002 – despite overflowing granaries – clearly show.
- To have access to clean water: as the privatization of global water supplies suggests.
- To be protected against cold: as the corpses on the streets of Moscow each winter would testify if they could.
- To expect shelter: as the street-dwellers of Mumbai demonstrate, as they sleep, eat and defecate in full gaze of passers-by.
- To expect healthcare: as the AIDS victims in Malawi and South Africa show.
- To be educated: as child workers in fields, factories and private homes worldwide make clear.

Traffic lights

In September 2002 the Traffic Department of Delhi issued a notification forbidding motorists to give to beggars at traffic lights. Many such 'beggars' are orphaned and abandoned children. This keeps traffic flowing and removes the blemish of poverty from the gaze of motorists. Any driver tempted to charity will be fined 100 rupees – 300 for any subsequent 'offense'. At a stroke, the Government criminalizes human generosity and makes criminals out of youngsters, who will turn from selling magazines, chewing-gum and toys at traffic lights to prostitution, drug-dealing and thieving. The children are already subject to police extortion, beatings and sexual abuse. ■

The war on poor people is dressed up in the language of 'progress': modernization, 'beautification' of the city, improvements to the landscape, more efficient methods of farming, improved productivity – above all, 'development'. Sometimes evictions are carried out for the sake of removing 'eyesores', especially when there is to be some important international gathering – a summit, a sports contest, a World Cup. The poor, it is stated, 'tarnish the image' of a country. This must be avoided, no matter how tarnished, sullied or corrupt the reality.

Within the city of Delhi evictions occur all the time. People are removed to barren spaces outside the city limits, with no amenities or chance of employment. They are charged a 'relocation fee' of Rs7,000 (about $150), which also encourages them to disappear. Abandoned in the urban wasteland they travel back to the inner city to resume the only work available – domestic service, rickshaw-pulling, recycling, selling vegetables. They get up two hours earlier, at four or five in the morning, and pay a bus fare of Rs10 each way. This lengthens the working day and cuts their wages by up to a third. Poor people are made poorer by the same governments that ritually gave their support in international forums to raising up the disadvantaged.

The misfortune of working children is compounded by those who are supposed to succor them.

The elderly, too, are victimized by 'clearances' and 'relocations'. In Mirabagh, West Delhi, rumors of demolition have further unsettled people whose lives have been a story of continuous disturbance. Those scarred by age and loss are threatened with removal once more for the construction of apartments or roads. Faces used up by work and anxiety, the thin arms of malnourishment, hands calloused by years of manual labor, joints swollen by arthritis: only the brightness of the eyes speaks of constant vigilance of the poor, always alert to the next danger menacing their survival.

The greatest burdens of evictions and insecurity are borne by women. Slum dwellers supplement income for the ill-paid police. Robbing the poor is, in one way or another, a major source of finance for officials, bureaucrats and politicians. Their incentive to eliminate poverty is small.

Who doubts the virtuous intentions of privilege and power which have taken charge of social injustice? The results are there for all to see in Delhi or Manila, Dhaka, Jakarta, Kolkata (Calcutta), Mumbai (Bombay), Mexico City, Rio de Janeiro – all the cities bursting with people trying to salvage dignity and humanity from the social wreckage of globalization.

Is it by chance that those to whom international forums routinely give priority – poor women, children and the elderly – are the main victims of economic processes which are supposed to uplift them?

Kimiyabhai

Aged 60, from Madhya Pradesh, she lives with her younger, unmarried son, an unskilled construction worker. Her older son is married, and she is not on speaking terms with her daughter-in-law. Kimiyabhai works as a maidservant, earning Rs300 ($7) a month. 'I weep because I lost my husband, and wonder what will happen when my younger son marries. Will his wife allow him to care for me? Where will I find my food? If they move us, where will I find work?' ∎

The mechanisms of impoverishment

Privatizing necessities

The World Water Council is a policy-making think-tank. Membership includes the World Bank, global water corporations, the UN, governments and the International Private Water Association. Five years ago at The Hague it recommended privatization as a response to the global water crisis. The Council endorsed a for-profit principle: water is not a basic human right but a commodity best delivered by the private sector. Protests against privatization of water supplies have continued in 2005 and 2006: popular demonstrations have taken place in Malaysia, India (in Delhi and in Bangalore), El Salvador, South Africa, Uruguay, Ghana and Nicaragua. On the other had, in Lima, Peru, poor people, exasperated by the inefficiency of the State, have demonstrated in favor of privatization. Privatizations can be stopped by popular action.

Occasionally, the depth of human privation reaches the Western press. On 1 June 2003, at the time of the G-7 summit, held in the French spa town of Evian, *The Observer* laconically highlighted the case of Sema Kedir, the mother of three found hanging from a tree near her home in central Ethiopia. The only clue to her fate lay in the shattered remains of a clay pot near by. She had collapsed on the final leg of the 12-mile hike from the nearest water well and spilled the precious liquid that would have kept her children alive for another day or two. Already in debt, she

---

Sanjay

On the streets since a quarrel with his stepfather, he has been a rickshaw driver since he was 14 – an occupation which wastes the muscle and destroys the body-tissue of the strongest adult. The effect on the unformed body of an adolescent is unimaginable. Sanjay's greatest fear is not of the police but of middle-class boys on drugs. Since these are not given money for drugs by their families they rob working children. Sanjay subsidizes the drug habits of privilege. ■

could not afford to raise money for a new pot: there seemed no way out.

Controlling the world's food supply

'The Green Revolution strategy is a text-book case of the industrial input-intensive method of agricultural production,' says the author and activist Susan George. 'It should have been clear from the outset that only the better-off Third World farmers with access to credit would be able to adopt it and that small producers would find themselves at a disadvantage. This is exactly what has happened. Competition for land has increased as agriculture has become a profitable investment. Rural dispossession has, as a result, intensified. While food production has indeed increased (although less than often claimed), fewer people proportionally are able to buy it and millions have been deprived of the means of producing food for themselves.'[5]

A more recent response to persistent hunger has been the 'promise' that the newest technological fix, genetically modified food, with in-bred pest resistance and higher yields, will solve problems of hunger. That the long-term effect on the environment, as well as on productivity, may be damaging is a mere detail; as is the fact that the technology will remain in the hands

---

Laju

Her son is addicted to drugs. She keeps the family by selling eggs from a stall in front of her hut. They lived in Delhi for 14 years before being evicted to a desolate area outside the city. Her husband was a rickshaw driver, a job which destroyed his lungs. He and his son now prepare food for rickshaw drivers in the slum. They pay Rs600 (about $14) a month to the police to be permitted to carry on their 'illegal' business. Last night the police came to arrest Laju, since she was unable to pay the bribe. A human-rights worker told the police they cannot arrest a woman when no other woman is present. They left Laju and took her brother-in-law instead: a form of hostage-taking by the forces of law and order. ■

Checked out

The Delhi Government recently published figures to show how much it had spent on rehabilitating people relocated to Bakarwal. Nirmala Sharma, of the Women's Awakening Movement, has a copy of the accounts. They declare 7 *crore* 84 *lakhs* [$1.5 million approximately] were spent on people from 3,000 huts demolished close to the hospital. All is itemized – money for land-filling, drains, for a children's crèche; a whole dossier of fictional expenditure. There is even a photocopy of the check, number 174008 dated 20 December 2000. The site is utterly void. Not one paisa of the money has reached the people. Government accepts money from foreign donors, charitable trusts and NGOs for the poor. No-one checks what happens to the money, which finds its way into the pockets of those supposed to administer it. ■

Personal communication, Nirmala Sharma, New Delhi, 2002.

---

of the transnationals that control them. No more effective device for decreasing the power of the poor over access to food could be imagined.

The flexibility of the IMF

Following criticism of the International Monetary Fund for the effect of its structural-adjustment programs on poor countries (there were almost 150 public demonstrations, riots or disturbances against structural adjustments between 1976 and 1992), in 1999 the Fund announced a commitment to 'poverty reduction'.

The new element was to be a Poverty Reduction Strategy (PRS) prepared by developing-country governments in consultation with their own people, as a framework for IMF and World Bank operations in these countries. This would end the practice of imposing an identical policy upon every country, irrespective of local conditions. Even the internal research of the IMF and World Bank showed that in many countries macro-economic prescriptions were not only increasing inequality but also throwing more people into absolute poverty.

It had been an act of faith that the policies of the IMF and World Bank would improve the position of the poorest. That they were ineffective remained curiously 'unseen', until the people themselves rose up in protest. It is astonishing how little the institutions knew about the impact of their own policies on the poor and on inequality: their own self-evaluation reveals the extent of ignorance and inefficiency. The Poverty Reduction Strategy of 1999 introduces two new elements: government 'ownership' of programs and popular participation, particularly by 'stakeholders' – the new jargon for the poor themselves.

Over 70 developing countries were required to 'design' Poverty Reduction Strategy papers by 2001. Debt relief for the most Highly Indebted Poor Countries was to be linked to this strategy. Debt relief, however, does not produce new cash to relieve poverty. Money that would have gone on servicing

Cochabamba

In Cochabamba in Bolivia, in 1999, the World Bank pressurized the Bolivian Government into privatizing water companies. It refused credit to the public company which ran the water services, recommended 'no public subsidies' against price hikes and insisted on giving a monopoly to Aguas del Tunari, part of the British company International Water Ltd, in turn owned by the US engineering giant Bechtel.

The new owners, granted a 40-year concession, announced big price rises even before they began operations. A popular revolt led by young-sters known as the 'water warriors' took to the streets of Cochabamba under the auspices of the Coordinadora (Co-ordination for the Defense of Water and Life), a coalition of labor activists, rural organizations, coca growers from nearby Chaparé, politicians, NGOs, local professionals and young people.

For two months no-one paid the water bills. The Coordinadora called for a symbolic seizure of the central city square – 30,000 people turned up. Police fired on the crowd, injuring 175. Martial law was declared, a state of siege imposed and the military sent in. A 17-year-old boy was killed, many were injured.

After that, 80,000 took to the streets. The water company left the country. The Coordinadora talked with the Government and agreed that the water contract should be broken. 'Now the water is controlled by the people' says an activist, 'the water is sweet.' ■

Marcele Lopez Levy, *Bolivia Profile*, Oxfam, 2001. www.oxfam.org

debt – some of which would have involved further borrowing – is not part of a pre-existing hoard, but would be realized from public assets, food crops diverted to export, and so on.

Forty countries have qualified for the HIPC Initiative. By 2006, twenty of these had reached the 'completion point'. This means they had, in the judgment of the IMF, shown 'a track record of good performance under IMF-supported programs, implemented key reforms and adopted the poverty reduction strategy for one year.

'Ownership' and 'participation' are treacherous terms. They help the IMF and World Bank avoid responsibility, since local (ie national) governments and the poor themselves can be blamed if poverty is not reduced. There is no sign that globalization is going to be significantly modified, particularly since the PRS must be undertaken within the iron corset of macro-economic orthodoxy. Concern with the old indicators – low inflation, exchange-rate stability – suggests this represents cosmetic, not fundamental, change.

Charles Abugre, a respected analyst in Ghana, says that 'if the PRS were a government-led process, why would the Bank and Fund send numerous missions to the country to develop the PRS? Why would the first mission be developed in order to ensure "client commitment" to the PRS? Why would the Bank develop a 1,000-page Sourcebook to tell developing country groups how to create a PRS, and another Sourcebook to describe how to develop acceptable trade policies?'

Abugre asks why indigenously developed national strategies should be negotiated with outside agencies. Social policies as an addendum to macro-economic 'efficiency', with their overriding emphasis on low inflation and reducing the role of the state, marks little change in previous policies. 'PRSs are empty rhetoric... a useful veil for the World Bank and IMF to continue their neoliberal agenda,' Abugre concludes.[6]

In the presence of these traumas, the role of international financial institutions only adds insult to the very substantial injury which the people of traumatized countries have already suffered. It is significant that since 2000, the emphasis of the financial institutions has shifted once more, so that the buzzwords of the hour now are good governance, accountability, transparency and the fight against corruption.

These goals are impeccable, but they raise at least two questions. First, is the uneven distribution of wealth in the world not in part a consequence of historic injustices, and therefore itself a form of

Niger's famine

In 2005, Niger captured the attention of the world when tens of thousands of people died of hunger. The precise figure is unknown. In May 2005, the Managing Director of the IMF praised the President of Niger for 'ongoing reforms to strengthen economic growth and reduce poverty.' A week later, the World Bank added its words of encouragement, saying: 'Economic management performance as well as social indicators improved substantially since 2000 in Niger.' The UN had warned late in 2004 of severe food shortages.

Early in 2005, rural populations were showing the strains that foreshadow extreme hunger – selling female breeding animals, eating seedstocks and moving to urban areas. In March 2005, the UN had appealed for $16 million to relieve (not prevent) hunger in a country where 80 per cent of people are subsistence farmers. In 2004, there was a grain deficit of 223,000 tonnes and 40 per cent of the 10,000 villages had reported total crop loss. In praising 'economic reform' in the presence of famine, the international financial institutions clearly demonstrate how far 'the economy' has become disarticulated from human need. ∎

corruption; and secondly, what effect does preaching against corruption have on poor countries, when the UK Government for example stops investigations by the Serious Fraud Office into money paid to smooth the way for defense contracts? In 2006, the most costly investigation ever undertaken in the UK into corruption over the sale of $6 billion worth of fighter jets to Saudi Arabia was called off, since the 'public interest', ie keeping Saudi sweet, was considered more important than the rule of law.

Foreign direct investment

One hope offered to the poor is foreign direct investment in their countries. It is considered a triumph for economies which attract large volumes of foreign capital to their stricken lands. The machinations of the transnationals are well documented. Insights into the way these operate sometimes create public scandals that move a wider world.

US companies avoid publicity over abuse of workers

in Central America, Mexico and South Asia by relocating to areas likely to escape scrutiny. By using foreign workers in remote places, exploitation may be undetected.

The transnationals and justice

In 2002 food giant Nestlé demanded $6 million from the Government of Ethiopia just as the country was facing its worst famine for 20 years. This was compensation for an Ethiopian business which the previous government of the dictator Mengistu nationalized in 1975. Nestlé declared repayment was a 'matter of principle'. A company spokesman insisted that conflicts should be resolved according to international law and in a spirit of fairness. The Prime Minister of Ethiopia had stated that 6 million people in his country needed emergency food aid, a number which could rise to 15 million within months. Nestlé's profits in 2001 were $5.5 billion.

The mechanisms of impoverishment

In the global market

The vast manufacturing capacity of multinational companies to produce all the merchandise housed in the great shopping malls of the world does more than take advantage of the unvisited sites of dereliction where they can abuse their captive workers. The great cult of consumerism sweeps up the middle class in the South as well as the North, in Bogotá and Tegucigalpa, in Lagos, Johannesburg, Manila and Hanoi. This has

---

The trauma of children

Cambodia has been subjected to the complex processes exacted by the Poverty Reduction Strategy policy. Rhetoric contrasts with reality on the streets of Phnom Penh. Laurence Gray of World Vision states:

'More than half of all Cambodian children are malnourished. Half a million between the ages of 6 and 11 have no access to education. Between 10,000 and 15,000 children are involved in prostitution in Phnom Penh.

'Cambodia has emerged from 39 years of conflict. The parents of today's children experienced the horrors of Pol Pot. The University of Phnom Penh's Psychology Department studied the mental health of children in 1999. The results give insights into children's encounters with violence, and reveal, for one thing, that it's not just economics that drives children onto the streets. The study surveyed 400 children between the ages of 10 and 12 in Phnom Penh and the countryside. They were not at special risk, unlike children from single-headed households or those living on the streets.

'Among the findings:
- 41% had witnessed domestic violence at home
- 56% had witnessed the beating of a close relative
- 3% had witnessed the killing of a close relative
- 20% had heard of the killing of a close relative
- 58% had been beaten themselves
- 42% had witnessed a robbery
- 8% had witnessed a rape
- 49% had heard of an instance of rape
- 11% had witnessed a kidnapping
- 65% had heard of an instance of kidnapping

More than 30% of female prostitutes in Phnom Penh are children. More than half of Cambodia's prostitutes were sold by family members or coerced, by force or deception, into prostitution. ∎

World Vision, 2001.

---

a profound impact upon the psyche of poor people everywhere.

If globalization reaches into every aspect of the lives of the people, how can poor people remain unaffected? When the poor become the excluded of

---

The Malawi crisis

The IMF was criticized in 2002 for its contribution to the food crisis in Malawi. Reports of famine began to emerge from the country in October 2001. It became major news early in 2002.

According to ActionAid, the crisis was compounded by flooding followed by drought, and by the Government, which yielded to the demand by the IMF that it sell maize from its strategic reserve and abandon its 'starter pack' agricultural subsidy program. The IMF representative in Malawi commented: 'We have no expertise in food security policy and we did not instruct the Government or the National Food Reserve Agency (NFRA) to dispose of the reserves.'

The country had had grain reserves at near capacity for three years. The costs of maintaining these and of repaying the debt from loans led to an agreement between the IMF and the Government to sell some of its stock of grain. Since prices were low the grain was sold at a loss. The IMF recommended reducing the stock from 165,000 to 60,000 metric tons by selling it abroad. The NFRA sold off virtually all the stock.

The IMF policy of privatization and reduced government involvement in the economy is part of a worldwide pattern. ActionAid concludes that regardless of who was most at fault for the miscalculation that led to the sale of grain, 'the IMF displayed remarkable insensitivity and ideological narrow-mindedness in the Concluding Statement of its Mission in May 2002, which resolved to withhold disbursement of $47 million to Malawi. While acknowledging the need for "urgent action to prevent starvation", the IMF statement failed to mention that hundreds of starvation deaths had already occurred just two to three months previously. It implied that the Agricultural Development and Marketing Corporation and the National Food Reserve Agency activities to minimize famine mortality were unjustified and "unproductive".'

ActionAid states that in the light of a famine caused, or at least exacerbated, by economic liberalization, it should cease to be possible to insist on a rigorous liberalization program at all costs, to ignore demands for a government's right to provide agricultural subsidies. Greater regulation of the market by the state and giving priority to preserving essential food-crops are vital. ∎

ActionAid, June 2002.

a global market, remedies for poverty become less readily available to national governments.

As rural poverty drives people into cities, they meet new forms of insecurity and uncertain livelihood. They are subject to arbitrary evictions, unemployment, extortion and harassment by police and officials.

The truly significant break between rural and urban life is that the latter becomes more totally dependent upon money. In the countryside, cheating by middlemen and growing dependency on industrial inputs for crops – fertilizer and pesticide – undermine the roots of rural self-reliance. The power of brokers and money lenders, the forfeit of land through debt or sickness, or for social customs – like dowry payments or traditional inheritance patterns – drive people away into the cheerless hopefulness of city slums: hopeful

---

Pago Pago

When Thanh Nguyen was offered a chance to leave her poorly paid factory job in Vietnam and work in one of America's Pacific territories, she saw it as an easy way to a good income.

But she found herself in a brutal sweatshop where workers were beaten and starved while they made designer clothes for the US retail giants Sears and JC Penney.

Last week, a court in Washington found Thanh's Korean boss, Lee Kil-soo, guilty of human trafficking. Lee... owned the Daewoosa Samoa factory, near the American Samoa capital, Pago Pago. It employed 251 immigrant workers from Vietnam and China in appalling conditions. They paid $200 a month for room and board, for which they received a bunk in a cramped 36-bed dormitory and three meager meals a day. 'We had one two-pound chicken for all the factory.'

Pay was routinely withheld, and when they went on strike to recover their lost earnings the managers switched off the electricity, making the overheated compound unbearable.

During the worst dispute, in November 2000, Lee allegedly authorized his Samoan managers to make an example of one of the Vietnamese seamstresses. Quyen Truong was dragged from her sewing machine by several men and a Samoan employee gouged out her eye with a plastic pipe.' ∎

The Guardian, 1 March 2003. www.guardian.co.uk

---

only because the seasons of wages appear more reliable than the pressures of self-provisioning.

The poor migrate to seek security: they wind up chasing wealth. But wealth is more agile than they are. It is better fed, it is healthier, it is more mobile.

Redistribution is now off the agenda, because the opportunities for wealthy people to avoid paying their due to society are so numerous – off-shore tax havens, secret bank accounts, the ability to move money electronically. Chains of concealment permit them to cloak their fortunes in anonymity.

Wealth never sleeps or stops. Its mobility has endowed it with magic ideological powers. It is taken for granted that nothing must interfere with the

---

Bananas

Last year Gildardo Zuliaga and 230 others lost their jobs when one of the world's largest fruit companies, Dole, decided to abandon the San Pedro banana plantation in Colombia's violent Northern province of Magdalena. As in most banana-exporting areas of Latin America, there is virtually no alternative employment.

Executives back at Dole's corporate HQ in California decided to shift more banana production to Ecuador, where costs are cheaper – mainly because there are no unions arguing for decent wages and benefits. In Ecuador child labor is common and so is lower pay for women workers.

When Gildardo and his colleagues pressed for compensation, Dole agreed to hand over the abandoned land to the workers, but refused to buy bananas from them. The workers set up a co-operative, COOTRASABAN, and are struggling to make a go of it. But as Dole has the banana business pretty well sewn up in the region, they have been unable to find buyers for their produce. 'Who do we sell the bananas to now?' asks Gildardo.

Meanwhile, World Trade Organization (WTO) rules are forcing the European Union to open its market almost completely, so it can no longer choose to buy bananas from smaller operators.

The World Development Movement explains: 'Multinationals like Dole are the biggest winners from the WTO's regime, placing themselves where social and environmental regulations are weakest. We need international rules to set operating standards and make companies accountable to workers and local communities.' ■

World Development Movement. www.wdm.org.uk

mysterious enterprise and effort that goes into the making of money. The rich are no longer monopolists of the necessities of the poor but wealth-creators without whom poor people would be even poorer. In other words, poor people now appear as dependents of wealth rather than as its antagonists.

Rich people are not objects of envy since they now share with poor people a common dedication to wealth.

Poverty changes. During the early industrial period Barbara and John Hammond wrote of the manufacturing workers that they were 'not citizens of this or that town, but hands of this or that master'. Of poor people today it can be said they are increasingly 'no longer the inhabitants of this or that country, but the excluded of the global market'. They are no longer the residue of the excluded of a national economy: they are the orphans of globalization.

Governments which speak of 'social exclusion' are avoiding a deeper truth. Since the great majority of social activities now take place within the market, what they really mean is 'market exclusion'. In Britain in 1999 the largest item of household expenditure became, for the first time, leisure, overtaking food, health and housing. The biggest industry in the world is now tourism, generating almost $500 billion. Non-participants in these core social activities are seriously disadvantaged.

Marginalized people are exiles of a global market. They may be seen in youths who, worldwide, haunt the shopping malls and *gallerias*, the great enclosures of merchandise and symbols of the market where most significant cultural and social exchanges now occur.

Relentless

This is not a feature of one country. The poor have been reshaped in the image of the rich. They have been subject to the same relentless advertising and publicity, the same urge to get, to have and to spend. Identical appetites and desires have been kindled for the tantalizing things of the world. They have seen the same breakdown of restraint, the same pressures as the well-to-do. But from the poor, the money has been withheld.

This culture calls forth among the excluded a caricature of market participation – crime, drug abuse, violence, addictions, peer-driven competitiveness, gang warfare. Evictees of a global market, surviving or perishing on the margin, the young become the mercenaries of transnationals, at war over logos and brand-names. Their obsession with emblems that signify belonging – shirts, jeans, trainers, accessories, mobile phones, jewelry – leads them to do anything to lay hands on these goods.

Their sensibility has been shaped by technologies from elsewhere, the placeless sites where things are now made. The instruments that transmit the music and images, the sounds and sights of the world are not created within view; manufactured in obscure factories, hidden workshops, the forbidden cities of export priority zones of Jakarta, Tijuana or Nairobi. The goods come into people's lives from the dark places of the world, cleansed of blood and sweat; shining objects ritually purified by the distance between producers and consumers – that no-man's-land of concealment, transformation and forgetting.

'Market exclusion' has always been the natural condition of most of humanity, in the sense that most human activity has been concerned with self-provisioning. Trade between localities, districts, regions of the world is of great antiquity. Empires have plundered, bartered or stolen from vanquished peoples. Local markets, too, are embedded in all societies and cultures.

But the institutionalizing of a 'global market' dates only from the age of imperialism. To live within the constraints of a local resource-base was not an intolerable imposition upon self-reliant peoples. But local markets are being usurped by their global successor. The integration of all countries into the global market leads to the disintegration of communities, the dissolution of belonging, the destruction of the places where people must lead their lives. And the poor, no longer a domestic residuum of the excluded, are human sacrifices to the monstrous pathologies of wealth creation – for which even the word poverty itself is a meager, impoverished description.

1 Anisur Rahman, *People's Self-Development*, Dhaka University Press, 1993. 2 *The Guardian*, 18 February 2003 www.guardian.co.uk. 3 World Development Movement www.wdm.org.uk. 4 The Bretton Woods Project. 5 Susan George, *Ill Fares the Land*, Institute of Policy Studies, Washington, 1984. 6 Charles Abugre, *Still Sapping the Poor*, World Development Movement, 2000.

5 Wealth and poverty

The cooked books of privilege hide the true cost of wealth: obesity, crime, drugs, forced migration, as well as the shadow economy. So what is development and does it bring happiness?

'We are not concerned with the very poor. They are unthinkable, and only to be approached by the statistician or the poet.'
EM Forster, author

THE MYTH PROMOTED by international financial institutions is that their actions are governed by 'economic efficiency'. The theory is that the rich must be given 'incentives' to get richer while the poor must be punished by 'deterrents'. We might ask: what 'efficiency' is gained from consigning poor people to ghettoes of crime, poverty and exclusion, while the wealthy live in beleaguered 'gated communities' of privilege, protected by bodyguards, police escorts and bulletproof cars? It may comfort the impoverished to believe 'the rich are not happy'. But is it true?

Tilda

Tilda is the wife of a banker in Rio de Janeiro. They live in a villa, ornamental grilles at the windows, spikes and razor wire on the high walls surrounding the compound. There are armed guards in sentry boxes and heat sensors flood the area with light at the approach of any intruder. Dogs on chains bark into the night.

Occasionally Tilda goes out of this fortress. Before doing so she assumes a disguise. She dresses like her maid. She puts on a plain dress, removes her gold watch, earrings and jewels, puts sandals on her feet and takes a string bag. She leaves her purse at home and carries in her pocket just enough money to satisfy a robber, should she be assaulted. Sometimes it pleases her to catch the bus, but she always stays at the front since robberies are more common at the back. Whenever Tilda wants to go out of her gilded cage, she must pretend to be poor. She rather enjoys this – it makes her feel like ordinary person. ■

Wealth and poverty

Wealthy individuals, too, suffer from the relationship of injustice, albeit in a different way. This is not an abstraction. It impacts violently upon their lives. William Morris wrote of a 'humanity wasted, in one way or another, by poverty or excess'. This was not a figure of speech. It referred to the nature of lives which enjoy the tainted advantages of a cruelty which separates rich from poor – that most persistent of the apartheids of the world.

This minor irritant in the lives of the well-to-do only hints at the hidden costs to rich people of global social injustice.

The cost of wealth

Compared to the miseries of poverty the diseases of wealth are generally considered a price worth paying. The balance between gains and losses – or, in the language of economics, costs and benefits – is rarely judged dispassionately. The social afflictions in the rich world are perceived in isolation from the others and are attributed to individual psychopathology. In this way drugs, crime, alcohol abuse, loneliness, psychic disorder, the breakdown of relationships, become private problems, as though unconnected with society. Yet patterns of disorder suggest that the costs of wealth are far greater than anything that appears in the cooked books of privilege.

The case of obesity

There is much discussion about increasing numbers of overweight and obese people in the Western world, particularly in the US: 61 per cent of Americans are overweight. A quarter of those aged 19 or under are overweight or obese – double the number of 30 years ago. The US surgeon-general's report linked obesity to 300,000 deaths in 2002, the second-biggest killer after tobacco. The healthcare cost of obesity-related illness is $117 billion a year.

That this is connected with dietary change – consumption of fast food, much of it with high fat and sugar content – is no secret: 35 per cent of food in the US is now consumed outside the home. In January 2003 two teenagers, Ashley Pelman aged 14 (weighing 13½ stone/85 kilos) and Jazlyn Bradley (21 stone/135 kilos), tried to sue McDonald's for making them fat. Although the case was thrown out, it suggests bad nutrition is an affliction of privilege.

Another contributory factor is the sedentary US lifestyle. People in the US rely upon their car more than any other people in the world. With the rise in hours spent viewing TV, and TV snacking and 'grazing' an accompanying activity, together with home computer and video games, there are fewer incentives for children to take exercise. Compulsory physical activity in school has dropped sharply. The US Department of Agriculture states that the food industry provides about 3,800 calories per person a day, which is almost twice the calorie requirement of women and 33 per cent more than men need.

The response to the heightened incidence of obesity is not any modification of diet or more physical activity. Instead, drug companies have been seeking 'medical' answers to the problem. About 30 potential drugs are being developed by the industry. This shows up in statistics as 'economic growth' – the supreme index of the good fortune of those in the world's richest country.[1]

Nothing illustrates more clearly how, when rich people monopolize the necessities of life, they damage not just poor people but themselves as well.

The social pathology of crime

With growing social inequality come increases in crime. In the US crime rates per 100,000 inhabitants went up from 1,888 in 1960 to 5,898 in 1996. In 1996 the crime rate was 313 per cent higher than in

1960. Crime accounts for more death, injuries and loss of property than all natural disasters combined. Approximately 13 million people (approximately five per cent of the US population) are victims of crime every year. About one-and-a-half million are victims of violent crime. Such figures suggest that in ten years half the people of the country might expect to have been victims.[2]

According to British Government figures, the number of crimes recorded by the police in 2001/02 was 5.5 million, an increase of seven per cent compared to the year before. Changes in police recording practice suggest an underlying increase of about two per cent.

The British Crime Survey asks randomly selected adults about their experience of victimization in the previous year. In 2002 the sample was almost 40,000 people. Crimes against adults living in private households amounted to just over 13 million. This represents a decrease of two per cent compared with the estimate for 2000. The risk of being a victim of crime shows little fluctuation, at around 28 per cent.

If 28 per cent of the people risk being crime victims in any year, this has serious implications for the form of development which the whole world is being urged to follow. One argument is that police recording of crime has become more effective; another, that there are more opportunities for crime than in the 1930s and 1940s; a third, that this is the 'price' of greater mobility, wealth and freedom. But crime and the fear of it suggest a serious impoverishment of the people. It is presented as a regrettable byproduct of affluence, rather than as a major blemish on societies held up for worldwide emulation.

In the end, of course, ideological arguments prevail. 'Human nature' is usually the culprit, as with any other negative aspect of privilege. Human nature, the theory goes, is selfish. Individuals want to get as much as they can out of life and give as little as they can get away with. People are greedy and egotistical. Capitalism alone knows how to encourage people to follow their selfish ends and at the same time benefit society. This is economist Adam Smith's 'hidden hand': when individuals pursue their private interests, society is harmonious and free.

Yet people are also altruistic, generous and kind. Defenders of economic violence who speak of human nature take a reductive view of the full human being. Far from describing human nature, they are describing the nature of capitalism. If you behave in accordance with its dictates, of course you will succeed. This has little to do with insights into the nature of humanity.

You can't change society – but you can alter your mind
The UN estimates that 180 million people worldwide – 4.2 per cent of people aged 15 and over – were consuming drugs in the late 1990s.

The US Household Survey on Drug Abuse found in 2001 that 15.9 million Americans over the age of 12 admitted to the use of illicit drug(s) during the previous month. This represents 7.1 per cent of the population, a rise from 6.3 per cent in 2000. Although the majority were users of marijuana (56 per cent), a further 20 per cent had used marijuana and another drug during the previous month, and 24 per cent some other drug. There are 1.7 million cocaine users and 1.3 million using hallucinogens; 8.1 million have taken Ecstasy at least once in their life.

The cost to the US of the effects of illicit drug use is estimated by the World Health Organization to be $98 billion. Alcohol costs $148 billion, including $19 billion health costs.

Most Western countries have waged wars, crusades and campaigns against drugs – drugs tsars and supremos have been appointed. Yet most of these high-profile undertakings have failed. They have

Rachel Whitear

In Britain, the image of the crumpled body of Rachel Whitear, found dead alone in a flat, syringe still in hand, or of Leah Betts on a life-support machine, appear on TV as personal tragedies: 'purposeless' drug deaths, attractive, young, middle-class people with everything to live for, introduced to drugs by peer-group pressure – 'experiments' which took their lives. The better-off fall into drugs through a causeless 'vulnerability.'

For poor people there is another story: parental neglect, abuse, cruelty or poverty determined their addiction. Deprivation is the 'cause' of the addictions of the poor. It is clear there are class distinctions, even in the toll taken by drugs. ■

concentrated on the suppliers – chains of growers, producers, processors, distributors, couriers and dealers – while the demand for drugs has been interpreted as a problem of weak or disordered individuals.

Most Western countries recognize that drugs have become an indispensable aspect of the partying lifestyle of young people. In order to minimize the negative effects of recreational drugs, clubs must now provide drinking water, chill-out rooms, medical personnel and anything else that will reduce risk.

When drugs are intercepted by customs or police they are quoted as having a 'street-value' of so many millions of dollars. Not 'market-value', because no-one wants to highlight the obvious; namely, that drugs are the supreme market-driven commodity and illustrate the workings of the global market in its most naked, damaging form.

This desire to protect the market is why the connection between society and drug-taking receives so little attention. The demand for mind-altering substances in the richest societies the world has ever known is the object of a taboo; to examine it might reveal imperfections in the iconography of global success.

What inner emptiness, what harsh absences, what voids are being filled in the psyche and sensibility of young people by the search for transcendence through drugs? This must not be asked, since it might pose the question why the richest countries in the world create such a powerful desire to escape from the privilege they offer. Escape is the basis of major industries – travel, gambling, constant entertainment and distraction, sex, addictions of all kinds. What satisfactions do these societies fail to offer? What longings can they not satisfy?

These troubling issues go to the heart of the way of life to which the peoples of the entire planet must now aspire.

The abundance of the West is clearly incapable of answering some basic needs. This failure drives large numbers of young people into forbidden consolations. Their privilege obviously leaves them needy and hungry. This is a curious comment on the aid, advice and expertise we offer the people in the South to cure need and hunger.

Wounding and killings by people out of their minds suggest an indifference to human life that is at odds with an official humanitarianism. 'In the wrong place at the wrong time.' 'The luck of the draw.' 'Gone tomorrow.' 'You have to put it behind you and move on.' In the US the second-biggest single cause of death for children and adolescents aged between 5 and 19 – after motor-vehicle injuries – is homicide and suicide.[3]

A better place

In any city center in Europe on any Saturday night the streets are full of restless energy, an aggressive determination to enjoy. Many people are high, some are drunk. Fights break out here and there. As I am writing this, last weekend there was a killing close to where I live: a young man was stabbed after a fight and died of his wounds. A makeshift shrine has grown up in the spot where he died. The messages on the cards and flowers suggest bewilderment and pain. 'Goodnight mate'. 'See you in a better place'. 'You were one of the best'. 'Why did you have to die?' 'Sleep well'. ■

Such occurrences celebrate meaninglessness. Here is another basic need undermined by this version of affluence. Newspapers call such murders 'mindless' killings. But when people are offered mindless entertainment, mindless leisure, when many do 'mindless' work, it is difficult to know why the violence engendered by such a society should be mindful or intelligent.

The ambulances run with their cargoes of mutilated humanity to the Accident and Emergency Departments. People damaged by this violence are seen as victims of youthful exuberance or high spirits, the search for 'fun'. Bereaved parents may find the idea of their children as martyrs to fun distasteful.

A basic need is to contribute to the work of society – a sense of constructive and creative purpose. Here is another major defect in lives of privilege. Society evolves with only minimal participation by the young, whose gilded alienation goes unrecognized for what

---

Janet

Singapore. Almost immediately after Janet came to take up her job as domestic worker her husband in the Philippines moved in with another woman. Since then her mother has looked after the couple's two children.

In 2000 the family began to worry that Janet's younger son was hanging around drug addicts. The elder son entered college in 2001 to study marine technology.

Through the twists and turns of her family's life 34-year-old Janet has always been away from them. She has come to terms with the physical distance from her sons. But while she is physically in another country, her energies – sticking to her work and her future goals – remain directed toward home.

As for her personal life, Janet – who married at 15 and had two children by the time she was 18 – has had a few boyfriends in Singapore, though she does not want to marry anyone.

Janet... one of some 70,000 Filipinos doing domestic work in this city state of four million people. More than 800,000 Filipinos leave their country every year to work in foreign countries. ■

Kalinga Seneviratna, Third World Network

---

it is. Their disengagement from politics (only 40 per cent of eligible under-25s voted in the British election of 2001) is deplored, but the remedies proposed – voting online or at supermarkets – suggest it is little understood.

There is no need to change the world since this is the best of all possible worlds. Hope resides only in more, much more, of what exists already. This disinherits a young generation. It leads to cynicism, nihilism and a sense of futility. The young are offered the opportunity to 'buy in' all the things which other societies have given to their young as a birthright – values, beliefs, meaning. These are now celebrated in the West for their absence; the resulting vacuum is called 'freedom'.

'Primitive' societies often countenance human sacrifice, a tribute of flesh and blood to savage, esoteric beliefs. By that criterion, those societies which now present themselves as beacons of enlightenment must be among the most primitive the world has ever seen.

Migration

Globalization has increased mobility. It has also accelerated migration. The International Organization for Migration estimates that there are 100 million migrants worldwide. There are 20 million refugees

– another 30 million are 'undocumented', illegal. About four million are smuggled or trafficked. The trade is worth $5-7 billion a year. By 2006, it was estimated that 190 million people – 3 per cent of the world's population – were living outside their country of birth.

The majority of migrants are poor, displaced by conflict and civil war, evicted, forced to leave home by poverty, social violence or environmental degradation. 'Development' destroys livelihoods and uproots people: 25 million people have been displaced by developmental projects in India since Independence.

Most migrations take place within countries, from rural areas to towns. The second greatest movement is across borders to neighboring countries. Only a small minority cross continents, yet these disturb the people in the rich countries disproportionately. Agitations against migrants, asylum-seekers and refugees in rich countries usually focus on claims that they are criminals or scroungers, taking away our jobs and diluting our culture. The truth is that they work for below-subsistence wages and provide a pool of labor to service wealth and protect it against wage inflation.

Migrants contribute to the economy of the host country at enormous costs to themselves and their families. The UK Home Office estimates the net contribution of economic migrants to the British economy at $5 billion.

The costs of psychological and emotional separation, the breaking of families, are borne by the migrants themselves. Whether what they earn can make up for their absence is a calculation extraneous to the global accounting system. Many poor countries depend upon 'remittances' for a large part of foreign exchange. But the rich of Singapore have their daily needs attended to and the customers of McDonald's in Dubai get their hamburgers nice and fresh, accompanied by the painted smile and the cheerful exhortation to 'Enjoy'.

Illegal migration

Europol estimates that 500,000 persons enter the European Union illegally every year. About half are assisted by organized crime, which makes $15 billion a year.

Illegal migrants undertake costly, hazardous journeys. Stories are common in Europe of bodies washed up on the shores of the Mediterranean as leaky boats sink, of people suffocated in container lorries, of stowaways frozen to death in the hold of aircraft. According to Interpol they pay, on average, about $5,000 for their travel. There is co-operation between gangs organizing the movement of people and those in the receiving country, which are often involved in prostitution or the supply of cheap labor.[3]

Kamal

He lives in a tiny flat over an Indian restaurant. Officially, two men share a rent of $1,000 a month. In fact, there are four. There is one double bed. Two usually work night shifts, so the bed is rarely occupied by more than two, although occasionally all four sleep together.

There is a cupboard for clothes, on top of which are three battered suitcases. Two plastic chairs stand on cord carpeting, which has been burned by cigarette butts. There is a bare electric light bulb, a toilet, shower and a small stove, but since they work in restaurants they eat at the workplace. They rarely use the electric heater.

All are Bangladeshis, working illegally for as little as $3 an hour – less than half the minimum wage. They spend nothing on themselves. They walk to work. Two are waiters, doing two shifts and sometimes three – a 24-hour day. One is a student, employed officially serving breakfast in a hotel. He also works five nights a week in a restaurant.

Collective living is cheap, even in central London. All send money home. Kamal says they do not quarrel. Privacy is not important. Each man thinks of his loved ones, for whose sake they tolerate these conditions, until they are deported, or have saved enough to start a business in Bangladesh, or can bear it no longer. 'Our lives,' says Kamal, 'are not our own. They belong to our families.' ∎

Wealth and poverty

Those who castigate illegal migrants claim they have come for the dual purpose of stealing jobs and, at the same time, abusing the social-security system. It is difficult to assess the contribution to society of the despised and marginalized.

The traffic in people

Outrage expressed at people treated as commodities is strange, given the way the West grew rich, not only on slavery, but on other tradings in humanity as indentured, convict or transported labor, or as rural migrants to cities in the industrial era. Human beings have always been the most lucrative cash-crop of all. Every year millions of men, women and children are trafficked worldwide into conditions amounting to slavery. Among them, many thousands are young women and girls lured, abducted or sold into forced prostitution and other forms of sexual servitude. In 1997 an estimated 175,000 women and girls were trafficked from countries in Central and Eastern Europe and the Newly Independent States, primarily to other countries in the same region. In addition, Western Europe and North America continue to be major trafficking destinations for trafficked people from developing countries in Asia, Africa and Latin America.

Targeting young women

Traffickers target young women and girls in countries where socio-economic conditions are difficult and opportunities for women are limited. In a typical situation, the woman responds to an advertisement or is recruited informally by an agent (often an acquaintance) offering a good job in another country or region. The jobs are ostensibly for nurses, hair stylists, au pairs, domestic workers, waitresses, models or dancers. Recruiters may approach the woman's family, or recruit her at matchmaking parties

Anna and Rashid

Sometimes we gain a personal glimpse into aspects of illegality that rarely reach the public press.

When Anna was diagnosed with multiple sclerosis, she was using a shopping trolley to steady herself when she went out. She was living in a one-bedroom flat in East London. One day she asked a young Iranian to help her across the road. His name was Rashid and he said he was studying. He offered to carry her shopping. She invited him in for coffee.

He stayed ten months and looked after her with great tenderness. He was also the last sexual relationship of Anna's life. She felt rejuvenated, desirable, above all able – an experience she had not known for a long time. She was happier than she had been for years.

Rashid came home most nights but occasionally stayed away. Anna understood he was working illegally. She accepted his comings and goings. Although more than 20 years younger than Anna, Rashid was excited by her: when she said she felt old he said when he looked into her eyes she was ageless.

He sometimes spoke of the debts he owed those who brought him into the country. Anna was on disability benefit and shared what she had. After some time he became anxious and preoccupied, frightened of unexpected callers. One day Anna noticed he had taken a small case and his shaving kit and toothbrush. That night he didn't come home. Nor the next one.

In the early morning Anna was wakened by the sound of breaking glass. The flat was swarming with police. Where is he? Anna struggled out of bed. They searched the flat and found some clothes. 'They belong to my brother.'

Outside, a small crowd had gathered, hostile to the police. 'Poor thing.' 'What's she done, robbed a bleeding bank?' 'Haven't they got anything better to do than ransack the flat of a disabled woman?'

She never saw Rashid again.

Not long afterwards Anna went into long-term care. She said: 'He gave me an extra year of life.' No matter what Rashid offered, whatever function as carer he fulfilled, the relationship he developed, this counted for nothing against the crime of outstaying the grudging shelter he received in Britain. ∎

organized by marriage agencies. In some countries, young women and girls are literally sold to procurers by relatives, 'boy-friends' or state orphanages. Some women travel overseas for arranged or brokered marriages, only to be coerced into prostitution by their 'husbands' when they arrive.[3]

Wealth and poverty

The women are captives, trapped in debt bondage, forced into prostitution. Often raped and beaten, they are confined until they agree to whatever is demanded of them. Their documents remain with their abductors and they dare not escape, since they are told that they will be deported or imprisoned and their family may be harmed. In the sex trade, women service multiple clients each day. Sometimes addiction is used to make the women more tractable. The Metropolitan Police in London estimate that there are 10,000 illegal immigrants working as prostitutes in Britain.

The shadow economy

There are no accurate figures for the share of the global economy taken up by illegal activity. How

---

Alenka

She told the journalist: 'I am from Timisoara in the county of Timis. I am 16 years old. I left Romania on 18 February 2001 and I arrived in Beserica Alba in [former] Yugoslavia the next day. I was involved in import-export between Romania and Yugoslavia with my brother (selling black-market cigarettes)... Some men came while I was there and they forced me to get into their car. They were Albanians. They drove me to a hotel in Montenegro. An Albanian bought me. He took me to the border with Albania. He drove me to a place called Shiak, where he sold me to another Albanian for 3,000 Lek ($200). This man took me to a hotel, told me he wanted to have sex, drew a pistol and forced me.

'The police came to the hotel and said I was working as a prostitute and put me in a prison. It was known as '313' in Tirana, the capital. After two weeks I was given a lawyer and went to court.'

The lawyer took her to a hotel and sold her on for 2,000 Lek to a man who drove her to Vlore on the Adriatic coast. She stayed with a woman called Vera, who told her she had a daughter in London. A friend would go with her to England.

When she arrived in London on a fake passport, Vera's husband Stanislav told her she owed him $4,000 for the journey. 'He took me to a sauna to work. During this time my name was Angela. I worked in ten flats and six saunas. I earned $500 a day or more. I gave it all to Stanislav.'

At the time Alenka was 15. ■

The Observer, 23 February 2003. http://observer.guardian.co.uk.

far this exacerbates or reduces poverty is unknown. Certain illegal operations are familiar.

Two things can be said of hidden economic activity. One is that, with the absence of any genuine programs of redistribution of the wealth of the world, criminal activity as a response to monstrous social injustice is understandable. The capacity of this to redress the balance is of course questionable; but the increase in global crime over the last 50 years has less to do with growing human wickedness than with the bitterly felt injustices of the world.

The second observation is that much of this activity shadows the official economy, takes place in the shelter of confidentiality and commercial secrecy, often with the connivance of officials and business. The criminalization of politics and the politicizing of crime support the redistributive effects of the black economy, and the continuing flow of wealth from

---

Noi

She left school in her Thai village when she was 11. She worked in her parents' fields. She went as a domestic servant but, with two friends, contacted an agent they heard would take them to Bangkok. She was 16. She was taken to a house where 20 to 30 women worked as call-girls. She met boyfriends from Saudi Arabia and Dubai who promised everything but delivered nothing.

Noi met a woman from her village who was going to Japan. The trip would cost nothing. They went to a hotel in Tokyo and, next day, a Japanese man came to choose two of the six girls there. He told Noi she owed him $20,000. The same evening she was taken to a bar where 30 Thai women were working. The customers paid $300 and had complete control for two hours. Sometimes Yakuzas (Japanese organized crime gangs) would come into the bar. If any woman ran away the Yakuza traced her and brought her back. Many of her fellow workers became addicted to forget the pain.

Noi was fortunate. Arrested by the police, she was deported. She arrived in Thailand traumatized and empty-handed. All that work had been for nothing. She returned to her village, where she works once more in the fields and also has a small grocery store. ■

Our Lives, Our Stories, Foundation for Women, Bangkok, 1995.

poor to rich – like the mainstream, which it mimics in caricature.

No account of global poverty is complete without noting these diverse transactions. Until more light is shed upon them, discussions remain hazy and speculative.

The consequences of such imbalances, however, are clear for the 'beneficiaries' of privilege, especially the rich minority in the countries of the South.

Off balance

- Trade in illicit drugs is a major source of income beyond official balance sheets.
- Smuggling or traffic in people is highly lucrative.
- There is a thriving trade in illegal arms, particularly small arms, which the UN says leads to 200,000 deaths worldwide each year in murders, accidents and suicides.
- The value of trade in endangered species – songbirds, animals, plants, flowers, butterflies and insects, timber and tropical woods, ivory, animal products for alternative medicine systems, bush-meat and other banned foodstuffs – is unknown.
- The laundering of money employs an uncounted number of people worldwide.
- No reliable figures exist for the prohibited trade in diamonds and other gems.
- The cost of bribery and corruption within and between transnational companies cannot be accurately estimated, any more than the diversion of aid and other charitable money. Kickbacks, surreptitious payments, sweeteners and commissions paid off-books for legitimate deals are not easily quantifiable.
- The work of mafias, gangs, crooks, slumlords, the running of unofficial welfare programs by drug-lords, escape economic calculation.
- The extent of white-collar crime is only suggested by spectacular failures during 2002, from Enron to Global Crossing to WorldCom.
- The unaccountability of accounting processes, the work of extortionists, kidnappers and those who hold others to ransom in one way or another have yet to appear on global balance sheets.
- The costs of crime – from street-robbery and petty burglary to spectacular heists and hi-jackings – remain obscure.
- Commercial theft and espionage, biopiracy by transnationals enclosing the global commons, stealing the knowledge of indigenous peoples, distort figures of growth in the 'global economy'. ■

The UN Development Program annually publishes a Human Development Index. Its list of what is necessary for successful development includes 'an improvement in living standards as well as access to all basic needs such that a person has enough food, water, shelter, clothing, health, education and so on.'

Two hierarchies of wealth

There are two standard ways of measuring wealth: one by average per capita Gross National Income (GNI), the other ranking countries by a combination of measures, including healthcare, education and the position of women, known as the Human Development Index (HDI).

Richest countries in 2005*

Country	GNI per capita in $	Position	Country	HDI rank
Luxembourg	69,800	1	Norway	1
Norway	42,364	2	Iceland	2
United States	41,399	3	Australia	3
Ireland	40,610	4	Ireland	4
Iceland	35,115	5	Sweden	5
Denmark	34,740	6	Canada	6
Canada	34,273	7	Japan	7
Hong Kong, China	33,479	8	United States	8
Austria	33,432	9	Switzerland	9
Switzerland	32,571	10	Netherlands	10
Qatar	31,397	11	Finland	11
Belgium	31,244	12	Luxembourg	12
Finland	31,208	13	Belgium	13
Australia	30,897	14	Austria	14
Netherlands	30,862	15	Denmark	15
Japan	30,615	16	France	16
Germany	30,579	17	United Kingdom	17
United Kingdom	30,436	18	Italy	18
Sweden	29,926	19	Spain	19
France	29,187	20	New Zealand	20

* Excluding small tax havens: Liechtenstein, Bermuda, Cayman Islands, San Marino, Monaco.

Wealth and poverty

What is human development?

The telltale phrase is 'an improvement in living standards'. No doubt this is uncontroversial for poor people. But as a measure of successful development it should be asked whether it applies equally to the seven thousand millionaires in the US. The assumption that perpetual material increase is indispensable to human development is not called into question.

In the rich world, social and psychological ill-being mounts even as 'standards of living' rise. The Human Development Index was intended to counter crude economic indicators of development. Yet the table of countries with a high human development index diverges only slightly from that which measures economic success. The idea is powerful; yet its application is undermined by timidity and reluctance to depart from the definition made by the dominant powers of human purposes – which remain, overwhelmingly, economic.

Hong Kong and Singapore are the only two rich countries missing from the Human Development Index, which sees New Zealand and Spain scrape in at the bottom.

This 'alternative' definition is narrow. UNDP is not going to report that, in subjective surveys of the world, the people who express the greatest happiness live in Bangladesh. This is too great a shock to received assumptions, which ascribe to Bangladesh a role of impoverishment, corruption and misery.

A 'World Happiness Survey' conducted by the London School of Economics in 1998 found India to be the fifth happiest country in the world, with Britain at 32 and the US at 46. Ghana, Latvia, Croatia and Estonia all came above the US. People in rich countries, including Austria, Netherlands, Switzerland, Canada and Japan were less happy than their counterparts in the Dominican Republic and Armenia. The least happy people were in Russia and other parts of the former Soviet Union, including Ukraine, Belarus, Moldova.[4] Of course there is a link between resources (or income) and happiness. In poor countries a small increase in income leads to a disproportionate improvement in lifestyle and life chances. Beyond a certain level, however, the direct relationship breaks down. Happiness in the rich countries depends on close personal relationships, good health and job satisfaction.

The point at which the correlation between wealth and contentment fails ought to be a focus of research. It might help those who are obsessed with economic growth to turn their attention to an alternative. If it is true that the excesses of consumerism are implicated in the multiple breakdowns of Western society this should, surely, be a spur to open inquiry into the possibility of change. Instead it is lost in silence, which dooms all humankind to follow an identical path of value-added misery in the process of global 'integration'.

Wealth and poverty – inseparable companions

Wealth and poverty are inseparable. This is unfortunate, since they are not natural companions. While sufficiency is not seen as the objective of human striving, obscured by seductive promises of 'more', poverty cannot be 'cured'. It can only mutate, constantly remade in the image of a particular and selective version of wealth.

We recognize in our daily life that wealth means more than money. We say someone has a 'wealth' of experience. We speak of a 'wealth' of detail in a wonderful carving or painting. We speak of the 'wealth' of the natural world – its beauty, diversity and variety. We acknowledge the 'wealth' of information contained in a book. We recognize that health is

Gilded children of the black economy

Conspicuous in all major cities of the South – from Dakar to Jakarta, from Lagos to Lima – is a new, assertive generation, mainly young men. They drive dangerously through city streets in cars given to them by their parents. Dressed in hand-crafted shirts and shoes, light-reflecting shades, rings and chains of solid gold, they are well-fed, with sparkling teeth and luxuriant hair. They have had the best of everything – imported playthings, private education, holidays abroad, video games. They do not distinguish between needs and whims, to which they give equal priority. Intolerant of frustration, they fly into dangerous rages if challenged. Since childhood, servants have picked up their clothes and placed meals before them. Restless and pampered, they have experimented with drugs, sometimes with disastrous results, as may be seen behind the discreet facades of private clinics in São Paulo or Delhi.

These young people, with respect neither for age nor wisdom – indeed, for nothing but the stark calculus of money power – are, above all, children of the black economy. Their parents have sought absolution through their young for their own misdeeds, the pay-offs, the corruption, the shams and scams, the false invoices, the speculation and shady deals which have enriched them. These youngsters are the offspring of employers of hit-men and blackmailers, ruthless movers and shakers, the pitiless functionaries of an economic liberalization that has legitimized the amoralism of privilege.

They have laundered their money through the blamelessness of childhood – as though it can be cleansed of the misery its making may have caused, purified by the filter of childish innocence.

But money transmits is own values in spite of the fortified villa, the lavish parties with whisky and strings of lights in the trees, the scent of blossoms that fall onto the marble softly as the footfalls of servants who exist to flatter the cravings of their cute, conscienceless children.

wealth. Everyone knows 'you can't take it with you'. We all come into the world with nothing and leave with nothing.

Yet the monetary view of wealth has imposed itself upon all others. In doing so it smothers all other ways of answering need together with the biodiversity and cultural diversity of the world. Alternative definitions of wealth – and hence, of poverty – can release us from this tyrannical and reductive process.

Here is the new global middle class. Its purpose is to police the poor and protect the power of those even more favored than they. If lawlessness and corruption are indispensable to their well-being, so be it.

The psyche of the children of black money is occasionally illuminated. A cinema owner is shot because he demands that a young man surrender his walkman as he enters the theater. A maid is abducted and molested in a car. A 12-year-old servant is dismissed because she is pregnant. Some young men accused of gang-rape in a slum area are said to be 'from influential families', which guarantees their impunity. Others set up a bogus movie company to lure young girls into sex. A boy high on drugs drives his car onto a pavement, killing three sleeping street people. A teacher is shot by a pupil who feels slighted.

Their parents are virulently anti-poor, the more so since the poor are many and they remain few. 'Our country is not ready for democracy. What it needs is a strong man. The vote should be given only to the educated. What we need,' say these products of unbridled indiscipline and social irresponsibility, 'is more discipline and a greater sense of responsibility. The dwellers in the *favelas*, *barrios*, slums or shanties lack character. You must have rules. More punishment. Caning for drug-dealers. Anti-social elements should be stood against a wall and shot.'

Sometimes they are called away to identify a broken body in the wreckage of the car bought for an 18th birthday; or summoned to confirm that a drug-damaged youngster in police custody is indeed the cherished child who wanted for nothing; or to pay the police to keep silent over the acid-scarred face of a young woman who refused their son's attentions.

Liberalization indeed. Everything running counter to tradition, culture and religion, from Colombia to India, Indonesia to Nigeria, is embodied in this new class, its celebration of lawless authoritarianism and disregard for social justice. ∎

Unhappy land

Despite higher incomes, better health and much greater opportunity for women, Britons are increasingly depressed, unhappy in their relationships and alienated from civic society...

An analysis of the latest findings from three pioneering studies which have followed the lives of everyone born in England, Scotland and Wales in one week in 1946, 1958 and 1970 – more than 40,000 people – identifies a society more fractured and individualistic, but where people still find their success, wealth and opportunity dependent on family background.

Fourteen per cent of men born in 1970 were likely to admit to depression and anxiety in 2000, compared with only seven per cent in the 1958 group in 1991. For women the difference in the same years was almost as dramatic – 20 per cent in 2000 and 12 in 1991.

Of those born in 1970, 22 per cent of men and 24 per cent of women admitted to being unhappy with their first marriage in their early thirties, compared with just 3 per cent of men and 2 per cent of women of those born in 1958. Single people too were similarly much more likely to be unhappy with their lot.

Voting has moved from a majority to a minority pastime – more than 60 per cent of those born in 1946 and 1958 voted, but just 40 per cent of those born in 1970. ∎

Changing Britain, Changing Lives, Institute of Education, London. www.ioe.ac.uk

Wealth and poverty are part of an ideological construct which, although it clearly 'advantages' the rich, nevertheless takes an unacceptable toll of all humanity.

Growing inequality in the world and the unsustainable nature of our version of wealth-creation has at least one positive outcome. It permits rich and poor to recognize that these extremes bring satisfaction to fewer and fewer people. It suggests the possibility of a new project of liberation from systems that subordinate the needs of humanity to the necessities of economics. It reinforces the coalition between young people on the streets of Seattle, Genoa and other places where conclaves of privilege go about their increasingly secretive

The experience of poverty

The Indian writer and campaigner Vandana Shiva sees a difference between poverty as subsistence and misery as deprivation:

'It is useful to separate a cultural conception of subsistence living as poverty from the material experience of poverty that is a result of dispossession and deprivation. Culturally perceived poverty need not be real material poverty: subsistence economies which satisfy basic needs through self-provisioning are not poor in the sense of being deprived. Yet the ideology of development declares them so because they do not participate overwhelmingly in the market economy, and do not consume commodities produced for and distributed through the market, even though they might be satisfying those needs through self-provisioning mechanisms.' ■

Vandana Shiva, *Staying Alive*, Zed, London, 1989.

business, and the farmers, women and poor people everywhere who are robbed, cheated and betrayed in a world which can easily supply a secure sufficiency for all its people.

1 *Financial Times*, 18 February 2003 www.ft.com. 2 www.disastercenter.com/crime 3 US Department of Health and Human Services, 2002. 3 Organization for Security and Co-operation in Europe, 1999. 4 www.nriol.com/content/articles/article1.html

6 Rescuing self-reliance

A potent idea is vehemently denied. The visionaries of decolonization. Grassroots initiatives in Brazil, Cuba, Argentina. Re-animating ancient dreams of a secure sustenance for all.

'When we were young we were proud of how much we could do with little money. Now they are ashamed of how little they can do without a lot.'
Woman in her 80s.

IN A GLOBALIZING world self-reliance has become an object of scorn. Any country or region which considers disengagement from globalization is accused of being backward-looking, yearning for a vanished past. Self-reliance leads to 'autarchy'. You cannot cut yourself off from the world. At best inefficient and bureaucratic, it leads in the end to the genocidal madness of Pol Pot or the ideological tomb of North Korea. Starvation and misery are the fate of those on whom it is practiced, regimes which know what the people want better than the people themselves.

The vehemence of denial indicates just how potent is the idea of self-reliance. It is the opposite of globalization, the centralization that impoverishes and concentrates wealth in fewer and fewer hands. Self-reliance informs contemporary efforts to revitalize the local economy, to rescue the homely and familiar in answering the basic needs of all. No wonder self-reliance is called 'nostalgic, backward-looking', fit to be consigned to the history books, like the economics of Gandhi.

Mahatma Gandhi's economics united collective with individual welfare, recognized the dignity of all labor, insisted that economic and moral values are inseparable, and were based upon giving new life to a village economy, where all people would be able to feed and clothe themselves. This was overtaken by Nehru's drive to state-led industrialization and more orthodox views of development. Gandhi contended that possession of anything beyond and above what is required for immediate needs could be seen as stolen property. He realized that equal distribution of the world's goods was impracticable but considered the rich should at least hold their riches in trust for the service of society. He advocated a kind of voluntary socialism. Non-violence, non-co-operation and civil disobedience might be used to promote justice. Such views lapsed in the environment of post-Independence India and, with the acquisitiveness promoted by liberalization after 1990, seemed altogether forgotten.

Another great visionary of decolonization and self-reliance was Julius Nyerere, who led Tanzania from its independence in 1961 until he resigned in 1985. Known as *Mwalimu*, or teacher, he is as widely revered as Gandhi, whenever heroes of liberation struggles are honored.

In the Arusha Declaration of 1967, Nyerere said the development of a country is brought about not by money but by people and their labor. He spoke of the vast natural riches of Tanzania, its capacity to produce maize, rice, wheat, beans and groundnuts and cash-crops such as sisal, coffee, cotton, tobacco, pyrethrum and tea; the land which offers rich grazing for cattle, sheep, goats and for raising chickens; the seas and lakes which abound with fish. He advocated harder work in gardens, fields and *shambas*. He wanted to equalize the division of labor, since women worked harder than men. Influenced, perhaps, as much by his Catholic missionary education as by a puritanical socialism, he deplored the squandering of human resources on dancing, drinking and gossip, and sought to redirect these towards productive activity.

To help people's abilities to flower, Nyerere proposed universal free education and healthcare. Since many people lived in scattered homesteads, they must be brought together in *ujamaa* (family) villages, which would make it easier to deliver services. Nyerere knew the co-operative spirit of the peasants, who often combined to work for one another in building houses, at harvest time, in festival celebrations. He said: 'We in Africa have no need of being "converted" to socialism... It is rooted in our own past – in the traditional society that has produced us.' He foresaw little resistance to the incorporation of these 'innate' characteristics into state institutions.

Perhaps he paid too little attention to peasant pride in ownership of a small piece of land; perhaps he didn't perceive that even nomadic groups were rooted in well-traveled circles, returning to the same places when soil fertility had regenerated; perhaps he identified too closely with ideological wishful thinking. Anxious to prevent the emergence of a black exploitative middle class, he alienated the prosperous minority that had grown up in the dying years of colonialism. These, along with many Asian entrepreneurs, left the country.

Gardens in Cuba

Sixty per cent of the vegetables consumed in Cuba today are organically grown in city gardens. With the disintegration of the Soviet Union, on which Cuba depended, the country lost access to pesticides, fertilizer and tractor fuel. This, together with the continuing embargo by the US, ought to have ensured the collapse of the regime.

That it didn't is a tribute to the creativity of people who have lived for half a century in a state of siege. In place of industrialized agriculture, Cuba has developed a low-input sustainable system. In the countryside organic sugar, coffee and orange farms have been established. But the real triumph is Cuba's ability to mobilize popular support for turning unused city land into small vegetable plots. There are now more than 60,000 huertos, or gardens, growing food in Havana alone. People have drawn on their memories of childhood in the countryside to revive old skills; and the people of Cuba, despite their poverty, now enjoy one of the healthiest diets in the world. ■

Walter Schwarz, *Resurgence*, May/June 2002. www.resurgence.org.

Whatever the internal resistance, Nyerere underestimated the ill will of an outside world, to which self-reliance was anathema. As the mantras of financial institutions – free trade, liberalization and privatization – grew more insistent, oil prices rose, income from cash-crops declined, and dependency on aid grew. Nyerere was pressured to follow other countries which had taken IMF loans. He resisted. His Minister of Finance, Edwin Mtei, resigned. Subsequently, Mtei worked for the IMF. He is said to have stated that in the IMF he could implement policies in Tanzania which, as a mere Minister of the Government of Tanzania, he was unable to carry out.

Julius Nyerere told the *New Internationalist* magazine: 'When I was in Washington in 1998, at the World Bank, they asked me: "How did you fail?" In 1988, I responded, Tanzania's per-capita income was $280. Now, in 1998, it is $140. Yet in those ten years Tanzania has done everything the IMF and World Bank wanted. So I asked the World Bank: "What went wrong?"'[1]

The values of Gandhi and Nyerere, far from having been abandoned, have brought new inspiration to a generation in revolt against the wastefulness and injustice of globalization – not in theory, but in living practice.

Cuba has shown that people who say social breakdown and violence are the consequences of withdrawing from the global system are wrong. In Argentina, that former model pupil of the IMF, the economic crisis of 2002 plunged more than half the people into poverty. Hundreds of popular initiatives have emerged out of the chaos, based on local, collective action, including barter. At some 30 *nodos* (trading nodes) around the capital, thousands of people meet to exchange food, household appliances, furniture and services like cleaning and hair-styling. It is estimated that trading worth $40 million takes place at these barter markets.

Rescuing self-reliance

People's assemblies have become an important means of organization in Argentina. They arose out of militant street action, the poor and working class *piqueteros*, who blocked highways and oil refineries, and the middle-class *cacelerazos*, who banged pots and pans and occasionally attacked banks. The *asambleas* are a response to the failure of representative democracy – it represents only factions of ruling élites, as in all formally 'democratic' countries. There were in 2002 about 80 assemblies in Buenos Aires alone. This is a truly radical initiative because it hints at alternative and more effective democratic structures than the four-yearly vote for unaccountable and non-representative instruments of the status quo.[2]

One of the most successful social movements in the world is also from Latin America – the Landless Workers' Movement in Brazil. Hundreds of thousands of landless peasants have taken on themselves land reform in a country where less than 3 per cent of the

---

Landless Workers' Movement

While 60 per cent of Brazil's farmland lies idle, 25 million peasants live by casual day-labor. In 1985, with the support of the Catholic Church, hundreds of people took over and established a co-operative on an unused plantation in the south of the country. They were granted ownership of the land in 1987. Now more than 350,000 families have won titles to over 15 million acres. In 1999 more than 25,000 families occupied unproductive land. Currently, 70,000 families are occupying land in anticipation of government recognition. Securing land offers people food security and sets up an alternative form of social and economic development.

In the past 10 years more than 1,000 people have been killed as a result of land conflicts. Few of the perpetrators of these crimes have been brought to justice.

The Landless Workers' Movement (MST) has the support of a broad international network of human-rights groups, religious organizations and labor unions. It has created 60 food co-operatives as well as small agricultural industries. Their literacy program involves 600 educators working with adults and adolescents. ■

Landless Workers' Movement. www.mst.brazil.org

---

population owns 66 per cent of the arable land.

Many of the contemporary movements towards self-reliance have learned from mistakes of the past. Walter Mgboyo in Tanzania said: 'We had self-reliance without development. Now we have development without self-reliance. We should understand that these cannot be separated.'

Many people, both in the West and the South, now believe that everything which can be produced in the immediate vicinity of where people live should be produced there, and trade limited to such goods and services as cannot be provided locally. Localism is a useful antidote to globalization, but not when it becomes narrow parochialism, xenophobia and distrust

---

Food sufficiency

Despite the image of constant famine, the food available to every Ethiopian is generally well above the minimum caloric requirement – even excluding fruit, vegetables and animal products.

In 1995, the Institute of Sustainable Development carried out an experiment jointly with Ethiopia's Environment Protection Agency aimed at stimulating four local communities in Tigray, Northern Ethiopia, to intensify production as they know best, but with composting being introduced as a new technology. The smallholder farmers were reassured that the government would not interfere with their decisions or their management of the environment. Each local community developed its own statutes.

The results were remarkable. In one local community it was possible to compare the impact of different inputs:

Comparison of effects of different inputs, in kilogram/hectare

Crop	No input	Compost	Chemical fertilizers
Teff	790	1,710	1,840
Finger millet	760	1,850	1,570
Maize	1,760	5,040	7,100
Faba bean	940	2,310	not used

Composting increased yield two to three times, comparing favorably with chemical fertilizers, and in the case of finger millet out-performed them. What the farmers have realized is that the effect of chemical fertilizers disappears – often even before one season is out – while the effect of compost is cumulative over several consecutive years. ■

Institute of Science in Society, 'Ethiopia can feed herself', www.i-sis.org/uk

of the stranger. If allied to an open internationalism, local self-provisioning offers a true alternative. But localization must also apply to privilege as well as being offered as a remedy to poor people.

In the West, a new generation is challenging the impoverishing dynamic of globalism, denying the fatalism of Western leaders, including British Prime Minister Tony Blair, who stated that 'globalization is irreversible and irresistible'. Writer Colin Hines eloquently advocates an alternative that opposes the prescriptions which keep poor people poor. He is for safeguarding national and regional economies against the import of goods that can be produced locally, localizing the flow of money so that it is directed to reinforcing the economies of communities, and redirecting trade and aid towards reconstructing local communities rather than towards international competitiveness.[3]

All over the world, poor people have themselves been reclaiming definitions of what they understand to be a good life. Advocates of global democracy want everyone on earth to become participants in world governance. Local initiatives of producer and service co-operatives are permitting people to dispense with the products of remote corporations. The New Economics Foundation has set up alternative indicators which give a more sensitive account of human well-being than existing economic measures.

The establishment of microcredit schemes has enabled millions of poor women to achieve a measure of economic independence. The writer Winin Pereira pointed out that the profitability of even the most powerful transnational companies would be wiped out if a mere 10 per cent of people ceased buying their products. Campaigns for fair trade, efforts to bring producers and consumers closer together, pressure-groups for unadulterated food, for clean water, for human-scale communities, for simple living, for greater

Microcredit – miracle cure for poverty?

Well before the award of the Nobel Peace Prize to Muhammad Yunus for the work of Grameen Bank, microcredit had been hailed as the great hope of the poor, enthusiastically embraced by NGOs, donors and neo-liberals alike. Microcredit involves small loans especially to poor women, which enables them to develop entrepreneurial skills and economic activities that will help deliver them and their families from poverty. Microcredit schemes – in defiance of banks and financial institutions, which traditionally refused to lend to those without collateral – have led to a repayment rate as high as 98 per cent from groups of poor women. It has also released people from exorbitant interest-rates of local money-lenders.

While microcredit is no doubt a useful tool for alleviating – but not curing – poverty, the extravagant claims made for it 'putting homelessness and destitution in a museum' in the words of Md Yunus, should be regarded with caution. It might be asked when indebtedness was ever an agent of liberation. There are estimated to be 10,000 microcredit programs worldwide, but their impact on the macro-economy and on poverty levels is less easy to trace. Bangladesh, where it began 30 years ago, remains one of the poorest countries in Asia.

There is always tension between entrepreneurship and sheer survival: although many poor women have benefited by financing small-scale business, especially in such areas as making and selling snacks, cakes, sweets and other foodstuffs, in tailoring and artisanal work, there are limits to how many such enterprises local markets can sustain. The use of peer-group pressure to ensure repayment also sometimes demonstrates the coercive power of local community. Loans may be used for consumption to tide people over a lean season, family sickness or natural disaster, and some borrowers have gone from one micro-credit organization for a loan to pay back another.

Microcredit has helped millions of poor people, especially women. However these are, contrary to much of the publicity, not the very poorest and not in remote areas. It is simply that a more balanced view of its ability to eradicate poverty is overdue. It is asking too much to expect loans for self-employment to overcome structural poverty, and unrealistic to expect it to have any effect at all on growing global inequality. ■

respect for the resources that sustain us, for greater humility in the presence of traditional cultures – these amount to a powerful popular movement against existing patterns of globalization. Such activities are not theories, but living examples of how daily living may be transformed in practice, and moved in the direction of a more just and equal world. The theory, if it needs to be elaborated, will take care of itself.

The answering of basic needs, security and purposeful livelihood for all people have still to be tried in the world: these simple, easily attainable objectives have been overtaken by displays of conspicuous wealth, which are both a caricature and a denial of them.

In the Arusha Declaration, Nyerere said: 'We are trying to overcome our economic weakness by using the weapons of the economically strong... It is stupid to rely on money as the major instrument of development when we know only too well that our country is poor. It is equally stupid, indeed, it is more stupid, for us to imagine we shall rid ourselves of our poverty through foreign financial assistance rather than our own resources.'

It is impossible to restore the sustainable societies of indigenous and aboriginal peoples. But the values they

---

Another world

The question remains: even if absolute poverty can be abolished within the existing world-system, will this be at the cost of even greater inequality? If so, this will only set up new pathologies and poverties, since global capitalism depends upon continuous growth and expansion for its survival. People must go on wanting, far beyond sufficiency, beyond satiation, even beyond superfluity, or everything collapses. At least two further questions then arise. One: how much more such growth can the resource-base of the earth sustain? The survival of one system may find itself at war with survival itself. And two: if two hundred years of economic growth still permit savage poverties to scar the richest societies the world has ever known, why should the poor expect to find their salvation in it? Can we imagine the evolution of other ways of answering human need? Does the present upsurge of popular resistance have the makings of a new paradigm, a different world order? Radical intellectual Noam Chomsky says: 'If these diverse, dispersed movements manage to construct bonds of solidarity and support... together they will be able to change the course of contemporary history.' This is what is at stake. It is radical, of course, but it also connects with an ancient and still unrealized dream, of security and sufficiency for all people on earth. ■

New Internationalist No 338, September 2001. www.newint.org

embodied – careful stewardship of earth, modest use of its riches, safeguarding the future of the generations to come, restraint and as high a degree of self-provisioning as possible – can reanimate ancient and still unrealized dreams of a secure sustenance for all.

Self-reliance, a more respectful relationship between humanity and its fragile resource-base, waits to be rescued from the condescending excesses of a global market which is utterly unresponsive to the needs of the poor, and which casts them, in its cruel calculus of gain, into darkness and silence.

1 *New Internationalist* No 309, Jan/Feb 1999, www.newint.org **2** http:// anarchogeek.protest.net/archives/00002.html **3** Colin Hines, *Localization, A Global Manifesto*, Earthscan, 2001.

7 Afterword

Since the first version of this book appeared in 2003, it would be good to report that poverty is decreasing. The economies of most countries have continued to grow – at the rate of about 10 per cent in China and 8 per cent in India. Instead of growing well-being, this seems only to aggravate the scandal of maldevelopment, particularly since inequalities have become more extreme. A recent report in boardroom pay reveals that the UK is now one of the least fair societies in the world. The income of the chief executives of the top hundred companies is 115 times the average wage, 249 times the minimum wage and 519 times the basic state pension. Fewer than half a million adults control nearly one quarter of the nation's wealth, while the bottom half of the population have seen their share fall to 6 per cent in 2002. At the same time, the press publishes articles – half-admiringly – stating that the super-rich 'inhabit a world the rest of society can hardly dream of. It's a parallel universe' (*The Observer* 17 December 2006). The wealth of Britain's one thousand richest individuals is estimated to have doubled since 2000 to almost $500 billion.

At the same time, warnings of global warming, the loss of biodiversity, resource-depletion, the chemical contamination of the elements that sustain life – especially of water – jostle with stories of the very rich. The contradiction between the wounded earth and the aggression of the global economy upon it is unlikely to be resolved by the Kyoto Protocol and efforts to reduce carbon emissions. Using up of the planet, with the waste and prodigality that implies, suggests that if we cannot deploy the immense riches of human resourcefulness more imaginatively, we shall create an impoverishment previously undreamed of, and which will make even the most sparing sufficiency seem a distant dream.

Appendix 1

Migrations

The debate over asylum seekers, refugees and economic migrants echoes those which took place in the past, within Britain in particular. Globalization is a replay, on the world stage, of efforts to restrict movements of people between the 17th and 19th centuries. These were abandoned only when it became clear that industrialization and the free movement of labor were unstoppable.

The rhetoric, and the attempts to deter people from leaving an impoverished home in search of relief in more favored locations, are historically familiar. If press and politicians know the words and phrases that will incite antagonism, this is because they already exist deep in the psyche and culture.

In 1601 the administration of the poor rates in Britain was placed in the hands of each local parish. Since some were more generous than others, many poor people moved to where relief was higher. Payers of the poor rate objected. In 1662 the Laws of Settlement were passed in order to prevent such movements. This reduced labor mobility and made it harder for the workless to move elsewhere. For migrant harvest workers to move they required a certificate from a minister of their former parish; otherwise they would be forcibly removed back to their place of origin.

This is repeated in today's recruitment of necessary labor from anywhere in the world on the one hand – and the deportation of 'illegal' migrants on the other. Britain is the generous global parish, the 'soft touch', the destination of all the scroungers and opportunists of globalism. The 'sturdy beggars' of the Elizabethan Poor Law live on in the proposed criminalization of beggars.

The Poor Law was amended throughout the 18th century, mainly to 'deter' the poor with the workhouse:

this is reawakened by efforts to deter asylum seekers by means of vouchers, or the abolition of a subsistence allowance. There is a direct line of descent from this in punitive attitudes towards those from the far-flung parishes of Afghanistan and Iraq and other distant outposts of the new global imperium.

In 1782 able-bodied paupers were to be found employment with farmers and landowners. Employers would receive an allowance from the parish to bring up their wage to subsistence levels. This foreshadowed the Speenhamland system of outdoor relief, where the parish supplemented wages according to the price of bread. It led to a belief that able-bodied laborers might abuse the system: the precursors of today's 'welfare cheats'.

Since the political and economic dominance of the West now controls globalization, the poor of the whole earth have become, in their way, our parishioners.

The laws of settlement were abolished only with the Poor Law Amendment Act in 1834. This made the regime in the workhouse so repelling that no-one would elect to go there if they had any alternative. This made clear the division between the 'rough' and 'respectable' poor − a distinction seen today between migrants indispensable to 'our' prosperity and unlawful economic migrants.

All this foreshadows the global situation at the beginning of the 21st century. Will we recognize the economic necessities of a system which has spread to the whole world the conditions contained within one country 200 years ago? Or shall we continue to impose our version of laws of settlement until the vast contemporary migrations of humanity set up by globalization, which we have imposed upon the world, compel us to do otherwise?

Appendix 2

What they said about poverty...

John Rawls in his *Theory of Justice*, published in 1971, said that a just society can allow differences in the allocation of resources – so long as the results are to the benefit of the least advantaged and there is equal opportunity of access. His fundamental idea of justice lies in fairness: this means no-one should be taken advantage of and everyone must agree that the rules are equitable. He spoke of putting on the 'veil of ignorance' before agreeing to the rules of fairness: this would make you agree to them no matter what position you occupied in society. It suggests the most advantaged might exchange places with the least advantaged – without demur.

W Runciman said in his *Relative Deprivation and Social Justice*, published in 1966: 'Political theorists of many different persuasions have wondered at the acquiescence of the underprivileged in the inequalities to which they are subjected, and have explained this acquiescence in terms of ignorance, or habit, or traditionally restricted expectation. If the least fortunate of society – 18th-century French philosopher, Saint-Simon's *"classe la plus nombreuse et la plus pauvre"* [the most numerous and poorest class] – were fully aware of how unequally they are being treated, would not all societies break out into revolution? "What is needed," said Durkheim, "if social order is to reign is that the mass of men be content with their lot. But what is needed for them to be content is not that they have more or less but that they be convinced that they have no right to more." In stable societies with a long and unbroken history of customary inequalities, it is not difficult to see how the aspirations of the underprivileged could be kept low enough for the pattern to remain undisturbed. But once the possibility of improvement has been disclosed, it becomes more remarkable that inequalities should continue to be passively accepted by the great majority of those at the lower levels of society. We must beware of confusing acquiescence with contentment; the impossibility of remedy can inhibit action without inhibiting the sense of grievance.'

Amartya Sen, in *Poverty and Famines: An Essay on Entitlement and Deprivation*, published in 1981, said: 'Hunger is best seen in terms of failure of people's entitlements, that is their failure to establish command over an adequate amount of food and other necessities. A person may have little means of commanding food if he or she has no job, no other sources of income, no social security. The hunger that will result can coexist with a plentiful supply of food in the economy and the markets.'

Indian environmentalist **Vandana Shiva** took issue with Amartya Sen's declaration that famines do not occur in democracies, when she pointed out in 2002 that starvation deaths have recently been widespread in India. 'People are starving because the policy structures that defended rural livelihoods and access to resources and markets, and hence entitlements and incomes, are being systematically dismantled by structural adjustment programs, driven by the World Bank and WTO rules imposing trade liberalization.' Shiva argues that political democracy divorced from economic democracy allows governments to come to power on the basis of hate, fear and exclusion; and that this undermines concepts of democracy that might link it to rights that include the right to subsistence.

Contacts

WORLD DEVELOPMENT MOVEMENT: a campaigning movement against poverty, highlighting unjust global relations and focussing on practical ways of addressing them.
25 Beehive Place
London SW9 7QR
Tel: +44 20 7737 6215
www.wdm.org.uk

ANTI-SLAVERY INTERNATIONAL: Campaigning against and researching on all forms of enslavement, bondage and abuse of human beings worldwide.
Thomas Clarkson House
The Stableyard
Broomgrove Road
London SW9 9TL
Tel: +44 20 7501 8920
www.antislavery.org

CONSUMERS' ASSOCIATION OF PENANG: Campaigning against global social injustice, and for equity and responsible use of resources.
228 Macalister Road
10400 Penang
Malaysia
Tel: +60 4 229 3511/3612
www.jeef.or.jp/EAST_ASIA/malaysia/CAP.htm

THIRD WORLD NETWORK: An alternative news service, focusing on the point of view of the South.
121-S Jalan Utama
10450 Penang
Malaysia
Tel: +60 4 226 6728/6159
www.twnside.org.sg

FOCUS ON THE GLOBAL SOUTH: Striving to create a distinct and cogent link between development at grassroots and 'macro' levels.
c/o CUSRI
Chulalongkorn University
Bangkok
Thailand
Tel: +66 2 218 7363
www.focusweb.org

JUBILEE DEBT CAMPAIGN: This is continuing the work of Jubilee 2000, campaigning to liberate poor countries from an overwhelming debt.
Jubilee Debt Campaign
PO Box 36620
London SE1 0WJ
Tel. +44 20 7922 1111
www.jubileedebtcampaign.org.uk

LANDLESS WORKERS' MOVEMENT (MST) Brazil
www.mstbrazil.org

NATIONAL ANTI-POVERTY ORGANIZATION
440-325 Dalhousie Street
Ottawa, Ontario
Canada
K1N 7G3
Canada
Tel: +1 613 789 0096
www.napo-onap.net

Food First/Institute for Food and Development Policy
398 60th Street
Oakland
California, USA
Tel: +1 510 654 4400
www.foodfirst.org

Bibliography

Abugre, Charles, *Still Sapping the Poor* (World Development Movement, 2000).
Bello, Walden, *Dark Victory* (Pluto Press, 1998).
Chossodovsky, Michel, 'Poverty in the late 20th century', *Journal of International Affairs* Vol, 52, No 1, Fall 1998.
Ehrenreich, Barbara, *Nickel and Dimed* (Henry Holt, New York, 2001).
George, Susan, *The Lugano Report* (Pluto Press, 1999).
Gorz, André, *Critique of Economic Reason* (Verso, 1996).
Khor, Martin, *Re-thinking Globalization* (Zed Books, 2001).
Madeley, John, *Hungry for Trade* (Zed Books, 2000).
Max-Neef, Manfred, *From the Outside Looking In: Experiences in Barefoot Economics* (Dag Hammerskjöld Foundation, 1982).
Shiva, Vandana, *Biopiracy: The Plunder of Nature and Knowledge* (South End Press, 1997).
Shiva, Vandana, *Stolen Harvest: The Hijacking of the Global Food Supply* (South End Press, 1999).
Rowbotham, Michael, *In the Grip of Death* (Jon Carpenter, Oxfordshire 1998).

Also recommended: Third World Network publications; *Third World Resurgence*; Consumers' Association of Penang, Malaysia; World Development Movement publications; Christian Aid; War on Want and Survival International, *New Internationalist* magazine www.newint.org

Index

Index